D1293970

THE
GARDENER'S
IRIS BOOK

THE
GARDENER'S
IRIS BOOK

WILLIAM SHEAR

The Taunton Press

COVER PHOTO: Roger Foley

Text © 1998 by William Shear
Illustrations © 1998 by The Taunton Press, Inc.

Printed in the United States of America
10 9 8 7 6 5 4 3 2 1

The Taunton Press, 63 South Main Street,
PO Box 5506, Newtown, CT 06470-5506
e-mail: tp@taunton.com

Distributed by Publishers Group West

Library of Congress Cataloging-in-Publication Data

Shear, William A.
        The gardener's iris book / William Shear.
            p.   cm.
        Includes bibliographical references and index.
        ISBN 1-56158-240-9
        1. Iris (Plant)   I. Title.
    SB413.I8S48   1998   98-5139
    635.9'3438–dc21   CIP

For Noelle and Justin

ACKNOWLEDGMENTS

While writing this book, I had to call on many people for help in gathering information, checking facts, and evaluating opinions. I'm particularly grateful to the subscribers of the electronic mail-list, Iris-L, organized by Tom Tadfor Little. Especially helpful were Scott Aiken, Ross Bishop, John Coble, Mark Cook, Ian Efford, Dorothy Fingerhood, Ellen Gallagher, Kathy Guest, R. Dennis Hager, Christopher Hollinshead, John I. Jones, Carla Lankow, Tom Tadfor Little, Clarence Mahan, Linda Mann, Maureen Mark, Sharon McAllister, John Montgomery, Diana Nicholls (Nicholls Gardens), Lois Rose, Bill Smoot, Dennis Stoneburner, J. Michael and Celia Story, Rick Tasco (Superstition Iris Gardens), Anner Whitehead and Lloyd Zurbrigg. Special thanks go to Mike and Anne Lowe, who contributed photographs, editorial advice, and wisdom from their enormous store of iris-related knowledge.

Rebecca and Amos Lee Laine allowed me to use their beautiful cottage garden as a backdrop for some of the photographs and very kindly permitted me to dig up and replant some of their irises, which, I am happy to report, appear to be thriving.

My principal photographer, Roger Foley, had only a brief time to take most of the beautiful pictures that illustrate this book. He did a terrific job, especially considering that the conditions during the 1997 blooming season were far from ideal. The following gardeners welcomed Roger into their gardens: Margaret Atwell, Rosalie Figge, Dennis Hager, Bruce Hornstein, Don Humphrey, Mary Ellen Kemp, Sheela Lampietti, Bobbie Lively-Diebold, Sarah Marley, Robert Pritchard (U.S. Botanic Gardens), Joanna Reed, Robert and Valerie Schultz, Brenda Skarphol (Green Spring Gardens Park), Dick Sparling, Dan and Ginny Spoon (Winterberry Gardens), Margaret Thomas, Oda and Chris Von Berg, and Carol Warner (Draycott Gardens).

Thanks also to the other photographers whose images accompany the text: David Cavagnaro, John Coble, Derek Fell, Mick Hales, Pamela Harper, Carla Lankow, Mike Lowe, Charles Mann, Brian Mathew, Sharon McAllister, and George Waters.

I also want to express my deep appreciation to the people at The Taunton Press. It has been a thoroughgoing pleasure to work with Helen Albert, Cherilyn DeVries, Ruth Dobsevage, and Henry Roth. They have contributed mightily to whatever may be good in this book.

Undoubtedly there are many errors of both commission and omission in this book. They are entirely the author's responsibility.

Contents

INTRODUCTION

"Why another book about irises?" a friend asked when I explained my plans for this project. And why indeed? There are probably more books available on irises than any of the other top five perennials in American gardens, and during the two years it took me to write this book, no fewer than four new books on irises appeared.

I had an answer for my friend because this was a question I had already asked myself. This book is needed because there is no existing introductory book about irises that is specifically keyed to American gardens. Fine, detailed volumes have been written by and for British, German, Australian, and New Zealand gardeners, but the only books that treat the problems Americans encounter in growing irises are long out of date, too expensive, or contain a great deal of historical detail that may confuse the beginner. That is not to say that these books are not valuable; they are, especially for the gardener who wants to move on beyond the information presented here (see pp. 166-167 for my recommendations). But the purpose of this book is to introduce irises to the American gardener, experienced or otherwise, who has just become interested in them.

Such an introduction is needed because the genus Iris is one of the most diverse and complex of all plant groups used in gardens. No single method suffices to grow all kinds of irises, and not all kinds of irises will grow in every garden. As you'll learn in reading this book, there are irises that thrive in deserts and bogs as well as in meadows and woodlands. It's a complicated subject, and the practical gardener needs the essentials set down in a brief, no-nonsense form.

In preparing to write the book, I read and reread almost everything in print about irises. I found many contradictory recommendations and opinions in these sources, so in deciding what to include and what not to include, I let my own experience guide me. I started growing irises as a young person in 1956. Since then, I've grown them in a wide variety of climates. In the mountains of northern Pennsylvania, where I grew up and first started gardening, winters are long, snowy, and severe, and the soil is stony and acidic. It takes tough plants to survive and prosper in the short growing season, since frosts may linger until early June and return in September. In Albuquerque, New Mexico, I faced a different set of problems, those typical of high-desert gardening—nearly rainless, hot summers and open winters that could fool plants into starting growth, only to hit them with a blizzard or hard freeze. In central Florida, nearly the opposite conditions prevailed, with mild, dry winters and steamy summers. For the past 20 years I have been lucky enough to have a garden in the mild, temperate climate of central Virginia, where it is possible to find or to create a niche for an incredible variety of plants. In each of these areas I've experimented with many different kinds of irises, and where my experience contradicted what was in the books, I've gone with what I've learned from the plants.

After 40 years of gardening experience, I've settled on three fundamental principles, which are behind many of the recommendations in this book.

The first is that the plants themselves have much to teach us. In order to grow them, we need to know something about their natural habitat so that we can find or create a microclimate in our gardens that will suit them. Seeking out and absorbing such knowledge will save you a lot of expensive experimentation.

Second, I don't believe in using pesticides, fungicides, and herbicides as the first resort when problems with pests and diseases arise. Instead, I advise following the principles of IPM (Integrated Pest Management), which uses knowledge about nature and the environment to work against pests and diseases. When in doubt, do nothing. Chemical remedies are fundamentally a last resort.

Third, my own experience and that of many others has taught me that a good garden springs from a healthy, living soil. You'll find repeated admonitions here to incorporate organic matter into your soil to feed the vast populations of beneficial microorganisms that dwell there, as well as the many tiny predators that provide natural pest control. Using too much commercially produced fertilizer can upset the delicate balance that exists in good, fertile dirt.

The Gardener's Iris Book begins with a chapter entitled "Meet the Irises," which introduces the major types of irises grown in gardens today. The next three chapters deal with three extremely popular and readily available sections of the Iris genus: Bearded Irises (Chapter 2), Siberian Irises (Chapter 3) and Louisiana Irises (Chapter 4). Chapters 5 through 8 take up other sorts of irises, grouped by their major gardening characteristics: irises grown from bulbs (Chapter 5), irises that require substantial moisture (Chapter 6), irises that thrive in dry conditions (Chapter 7), and irises for woodlands, for winter blooming, and other interesting and unusual situations (Chapter 8). Finally, Chapter 9 very briefly introduces methods that can be used to hybridize your own iris varieties and grow them to maturity from seeds.

Along the way, sidebars set off from the main text illuminate such subjects as particular iris species, special techniques, and useful iris relatives. A short set of appendices discusses societies where you can meet like-minded iris enthusiasts, recommends varieties to try, and lists some nurseries that specialize in irises. You will also find an annotated bibliography, a couple of computer resources, and an index. Photo credits appear on the last page of the book.

At the risk of giving offense to my many good friends who are iris enthusiasts, it's pointless to maintain that irises are easy to grow. No plant can be set in the ground and forgotten; our gardens are artificial ecosystems and as such need constant attention and maintainance. Iris gardens are no exception—to say otherwise only creates expectations that can never be fulfilled. That said, I want to emphasize that there are few plants that are as rewarding as irises. Their almost endless diversity and adaptability fascinate, and provide exciting challenges for every gardener from the novice to the most expert. It's my hope that this book will provide a starting point.

1

MEET THE IRISES

The Parts of an Iris Flower

Leaves, Stems, and Roots

A Guided Tour of the Genus *Iris*

Spread by the liberal hand of nature across the northern temperate zone, irises of many kinds grace habitats from swamps and lake margins to stony deserts and alpine mountain slopes. Best known to gardeners are the vigorous, easily grown Tall Bearded Irises with large, brilliant flowers and pointed blue-green leaves. These plants are found in nearly every garden, and sometimes you see them along roadsides or in abandoned fields.

To those in the know, the word "iris" conjures up a multitude of forms, from the tiny Reticulatas that bloom with the crocuses to the almost dinner-plate-sized flowers of the double Japanese irises that bloom in summer atop 4-ft. stems. In between is an extraordinary range of plant and flower forms, including species and hybrids adapted to a great range of conditions. All of these forms are readily available to home gardeners, and many of them have proven irresistible to the plant collector.

4

Clumps of bearded irises naturalized along the roadside. This is probably *Iris pallida*.

In this chapter, we'll look first at the structure of the iris flower and plant, then take a brief guided tour of the genus *Iris*. (If you're unfamiliar with botanical nomenclature, you might take a moment to read the sidebar on pp. 8-9, where words such as "genus" and other key terms are explained.)

The genus *Iris* contains between 125 and 300 species (depending on the authority), and it is placed by botanists, with other genera, in the family Iridaceae. Most of the plants in this family, which includes such favorite garden plants as *Crocus, Gladiolus, Tigridia,* and *Freesia,* have colorful flowers with six broad petals.

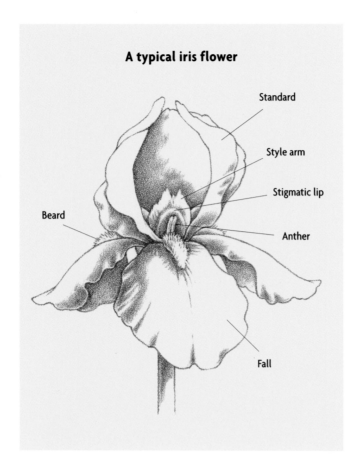

A typical iris flower

Standard

Style arm

Stigmatic lip

Beard

Anther

Fall

The Parts of an Iris Flower

Irises are characterized by a distinctive arrangement of their petals (drawing, left). The three outer petals flex back toward the flower stem as they open, and thus arch downward, while the inner three stay upright. The arching petals are called **falls,** and the upright ones are called **standards.** It is these two sets of petals that provide most of the color impact of an iris in the garden.

Within the genus there are variant arrangements. One departure that is often seen, especially in Japanese irises, is the replacement of the standards by one or more extra sets of falls, producing a flower that is essentially flat, or with a tuft of petals in the center. Another departure is the disappearance altogether of the standards.

At far left, the beard of a bearded iris ('Beverly Sills'). The falls of a beardless iris _(I. lactea,_ at left) are smooth.

The first step in classifying an iris can be taken by looking closely at the falls (photos, facing page). If there is a dense, elongate tuft of hairs near the base of the fall, you're dealing with a bearded iris; the absence of the beard (appropriately enough) marks a beardless iris.

If you look more closely at the flower of, say, a Tall Bearded hybrid, you will see three additional structures, also colorful, curving out over the falls. These are the **style arms,** the female reproductive parts of the flower. Each style arm ends in an upturned crest, at the base of which is a small shelf, called the **stigmatic lip.** In order for the iris flower to produce seeds, pollen must find its way to this lip. Speaking of pollen, the **anthers,** or pollen-carrying structures, can be seen just under the style arms if you lift them up slightly. The pollen may be white, yellowish, or even blue, but makes no meaningful contribution to the beauty of the bloom.

The falls, standards, and style arms are all joined at their bases into a narrow tube that expands into an **ovary** (which will become a seed pod if the eggs it contains are fertilized by pollen). The ovary is itself attached to the stem and protected by a pair of green, leaf-like **bracts.**

Leaves, Stems, and Roots

Though all iris flowers are roughly similar, the plants on which they grow may appear quite different. For a start, look downward from the Tall Bearded Iris flower you've been examining at the plant that produced it. If it's a good

modern variety, the stem carrying the flower will be about 3 ft. tall and will have at least three branches. Each branch will carry two or three buds; the successive opening of these buds determines the length of time the plant will be in bloom.

The stem springs from the center of a **fan** of leaves (drawing, below). Each leaf is typically a couple of inches wide and a foot or two long,

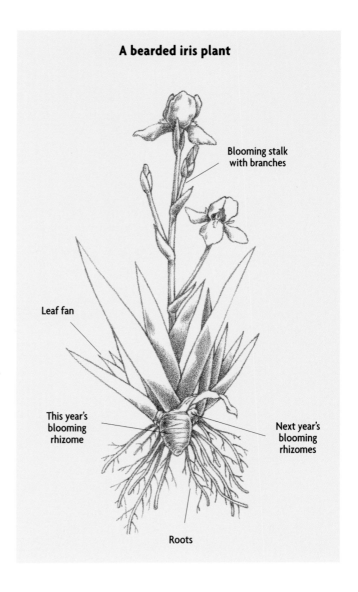

A bearded iris plant

Blooming stalk with branches

Leaf fan

This year's blooming rhizome

Next year's blooming rhizomes

Roots

tapering to a point. The arrangement of the leaves is worth noting—they are produced from alternate sides of the fan, and the outer ones sheathe those that are toward the center.

Now kneel down, and gently scrape away a little of the soil at the base of the fan. You'll see that it's growing from a rather lumpy, brown-skinned structure that lies just under the surface of the soil or perhaps even appears to creep over the surface. This is the **rhizome.** As much as it may look like a thickened root (and gardeners often talk of iris "roots" when they really mean rhizomes), it's actually considered to be a stem.

As the iris rhizome grows along the surface of the soil or just beneath it, leaves sprout from the upper side, forming the fan, and long, cord-like roots grow from the lower side (wait until it's time to dig up and replant some of your irises to examine the roots).

THE ROLE OF THE RHIZOME

The rhizome plays an important part in the life of the iris plant. It serves not only as a place for food storage, enabling the plant to get off to a quick start each spring, but is also the main way in which the iris can multiply, aside from seed production.

UNDERSTANDING BOTANICAL NAMES

More than 200 years ago, botanists developed a system for naming plants that ensured that each plant would receive a unique name, usually a two-part indication of genus and species. Plant species populations are recognized on the basis of their unique characteristics that set them apart from other such populations. These characteristics develop because, under the usual natural conditions, a member of one **species** cannot interbreed with a member of a different species. However, a number of related species may have descended from a common ancestor and show similarities that come from this relationship. Groups of related species that shared a common ancestor are placed in the same genus of plants. A **genus** (plural: genera) is therefore a group of species that are similar to one another and are more or less closely related.

To indicate relationships in more detail, botanists may also group species within a genus, recognizing subgenera, sections, and series. Thus a genus may contain several subgenera (six within the genus *Iris*, including *Limniris* for all beardless irises growing from rhizomes, and *Hermodactyloides* for the Reticulata Irises), a **subgenus** may contain a number of sections, and each **section** may contain several **series.** In a large genus like *Iris*, some authorities further break sections and series down into subsections and subseries. While it all sounds a bit daunting and confusing to the gardener, it need not be. Think of it as a kind of filing system, in which the species are the letters or papers to be filed. First they may be sorted out into folders (series or sections), and the folders placed into file drawers (subgenera); the drawers make up a cabinet (genus). To find any given letter (species) one first locates the cabinet, then the proper drawer, then the folder. So, just like a filing system, the system of classification makes it easier to find information regarding a species and its relationships.

Single rhizomes are active only until they produce a bloomstalk, usually just a year. After the stalk is finished flowering, that rhizome becomes inactive. Buds along its length begin to grow and branch out to form new rhizomes that will produce a bloomstalk the following year.

All the rhizomes in a clump of irises may be joined to each other, but each individual rhizome is capable of surviving and generating a new plant when it is separated from the others. In fact, that's how gardeners and commercial growers multiply their favorite plants. Irises are prolific in budding off new rhizomes, so new hybrids can be brought to market quickly and in quantities that ensure relatively low prices.

By splitting off rhizomes, home gardeners can share their new acquisitions with friends after just one year.

IRISES THAT GROW FROM BULBS

Many irises do not have rhizomes at all, but instead grow from a **bulb.** Bulbs and rhizomes are quite different from one another, and the difference is worth paying attention to because it provides important clues about how to treat the plants in the garden. A good example of a bulbous iris is the well-known Dutch Iris. These are the irises you get when you order them as cut flowers from a florist, and millions are raised each year for this purpose.

Plant names often indicate something about the characteristics or discoverer of the plants, and each plant in a genus has a unique species name. For example, we know that *Iris virginica* is a member of the genus *Iris,* and that it is common in Virginia *(virginica* means "of Virginia"). By convention, only the genus name is capitalized, and the whole name is in italics when printed on a page. (When typed or written longhand, the name should be underlined.) As long as the reference is clear, the genus name can be abbreviated to its first letter (*I. virginica*).

When plant species are adopted into cultivation, variations often appear, and those that are deemed worthy of attention are given informal status as **varieties.** Varietal names are not italicized and should be placed in single quotation marks—for example, *Iris virginica* 'Dottie's Double'.

Though species rarely interbreed, or cross, in nature, human intervention can break down this barrier and create **hybrids.** A hybrid is an individual plant that is the offspring of parents that belong to different species. Hybrids are often dead ends genetically because they themselves are sterile, but fertile hybrids can be further crossed among themselves and with their parents. The Tall Bearded Iris hybrids are the result of many generations of such work. Sometimes hybrid populations are given botanical names, as in the case of hybrids between *I. virginica* and *I. versicolor,* which are called *Iris* × *robusta.* A variety selected from among these hybrids is *Iris* × *robusta* 'Gerald Darby'. However, because the ancestry of the Tall Bearded hybrids is complex and because long names get cumbersome when the context is understood, varietal names are simply given by the breeder, as in 'Victoria Falls' or 'Beverly Sills'.

To avoid duplication of varietal names and the confusion that would follow, the American Iris Society registers the names of new hybrids; duplicate names are not permitted. According to rules set up by the Society, a name remains valid only if the variety is formally offered for sale.

If you were to follow the leaf fan of a Dutch Iris plant underground, you'd see that about 4 in. beneath the soil surface the leaves spring from a pear-shaped object covered with a tough, dry skin (drawing, below). I don't recommend wasting an iris bulb to see the internal structure—you can get the same information by slicing an onion in half lengthwise. The bulb of an iris is composed of a mass of thick, fleshy leaves (the **scales**) sprouting from a very small **basal stem** shaped like a miniature hockey puck. From the underside of the bulb's small stem sprout roots, though these are present only when the plant is actively growing.

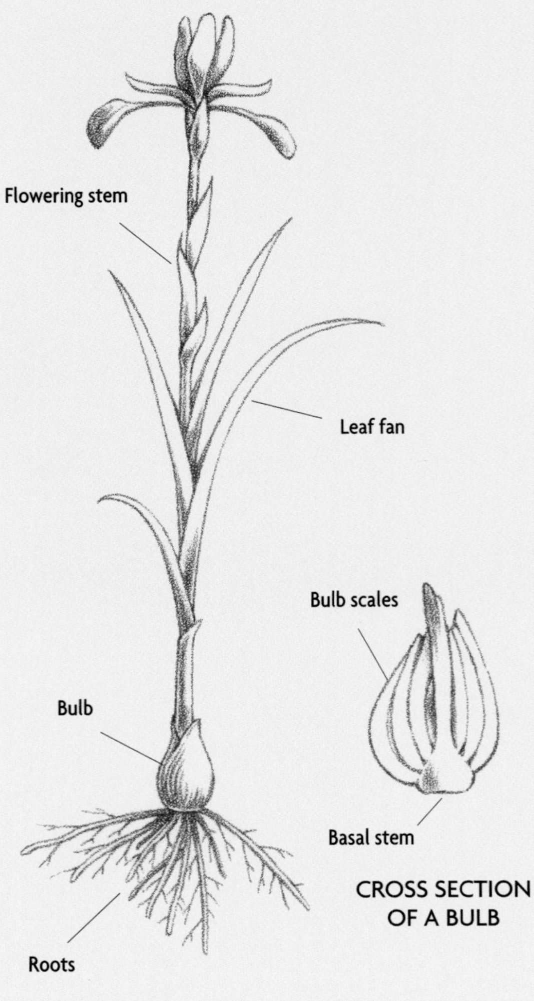

A bulb is something like a time machine, capable of a period of suspended animation. The scales of the bulb store food and water, allowing the plant to survive tough times, such as dry or cold seasons, and to begin to grow rapidly and vigorously when conditions improve.

A Guided Tour of the Genus *Iris*

With this basic information in hand, let's look at the plants within the major groupings. Specialists who already know irises well will find some of the lesser sorts missing from the list, and these are deliberate omissions. They are not discussed here because they are not readily available to gardeners or because they are exceedingly difficult to grow.

As you will see in the remainder of this chapter, there is an extraordinary variety of irises, enough to keep even the most fanatical plant collector busy for decades. In the chapters that follow, you'll learn how to grow all these kinds— when and where to plant them, how to care for them, and how to protect them from diseases and pests.

A bulbous iris plant

Flowering stem

Leaf fan

Bulb scales

Bulb

Basal stem

CROSS SECTION OF A BULB

Roots

BEARDED IRISES

For most American gardeners, iris means Bearded Iris. Widely adaptable, readily available and incredibly varied, Bearded Irises are by far the most popular of all iris types. And no wonder—the typical Tall Bearded Iris hybrids sport huge, colorful, fantastically formed flowers on stems that are 3 ft. to 4 ft. long. Everyone recognizes them. But for the enthusiast who is willing to delve a little deeper, the world of Bearded Irises holds many rich rewards from the aforementioned giants of the genus down to tiny, early-blooming dwarfs only a few inches tall.

This great range of sizes came about through the work of breeders, who combined the tall, robust species that bloom in late spring and early summer with early-blooming dwarf species. In essence, iris growers in the South sent along pollen from the tall species to friends farther north when the early dwarf species were just starting to bloom, and growers in the North reciprocated by sending dwarf pollen at the time the tall varieties were blooming in the South. Seeds resulted, and the new hybrids combined the flower size, stem height, and blooming time of both parents. These hybrids were then crossed with each other and with their parents to produce more variants. With time, all sorts of combinations came into existence. Eventually, the American Iris Society brought order out of the confusion by establishing a classification system based on the height of the stem, the size of the flower, and the season of bloom.

The American Iris Society groupings

The smallest bearded irises are the **Miniature Dwarfs** (photo, below). Their flower stems are about 8 in. or less in height (formally, the limit

Iris pumila **is the progenitor of the Miniature Dwarf Bearded Irises.**

is set at 20cm), and the stems are rarely if ever branched. The flowers are usually small (less than 3 in. across), which nonetheless seems quite large for the stems. Miniature Dwarfs bloom early, usually with or just after the hybrid Dutch crocuses. Most varieties multiply rapidly and produce vivid, if short-lived, sheets of color. Miniature Dwarfs do best in northern climates; they have inherited a need for a definite cold period in order to bloom properly.

Next come the **Standard Dwarfs** (photo, below). From 8 in. to 15 in. (21cm to 40cm) tall, these plants have flowers that are a little larger than those of the Miniature Dwarfs, and

they bloom somewhat later, often with tulips and daffodils. Their season of bloom can be longer because the stems are usually branched, with four to six flowers opening in succession. The Standard Dwarfs, along with the next three categories, are sometimes collectively referred to as **Medians.**

Intermediates (photo at top left, facing page) should be from about 16 in. to 27 in. tall (41cm to 70cm), with 4-in. to 5-in. flowers, blooming just ahead of the Tall Bearded Irises. Some confusion can exist between these plants and those of the **Border** category (photo at top right, facing page); Border Bearded Irises, however, bloom along with the Tall Bearded Irises, while the Intermediates flower well before.

The fourth Median category is that of the **Miniature Talls,** which are from 16 in. to 25 in. (41cm to 68cm) tall, but have significantly smaller flowers than either the Intermediates or Border Bearded Irises. Miniature Tall flowers are only 2 in. or 3 in. across and held on quite slender stems (bottom photo, facing page). The effect is delicate and graceful, unlike the other Medians, whose stouter stems and larger flowers speak to their vigor in the garden. Height alone does not define the Miniature Talls, but an overall effect created by a rigorous adherence to strict standards of stature, flower size, and refinement of stem. They should in all respects live up to their name as true miniatures of the Tall Bearded Irises.

Last come the **Tall Bearded Irises** (or TBs, as they are called by those in the know), with bloom stems 28 in. (71cm) or taller, and

Standard Dwarf Bearded Irises have taller forms as well as *Iris pumila* in their ancestry. This is 'Pilgrim's Choice'.

'Apricot Frosty' (above) is a Border Bearded Iris hybrid with color that carries all across the garden.

Intermediate Bearded Irises such as 'Honey Glazed' (above) are intermediate in both bloom time and stature.

Miniature Tall Bearded Irises (right) show graceful, well-proportioned form on smaller plants. 'Welch's Reward' is a much-refined version of the species *Iris variegata,* which is in the ancestry of many Miniature Talls.

This planting of Standard Tall Bearded Irises resembles a living rainbow.

flowers as large as 7 in. across. These are the last of the bearded irises to bloom. Literally thousands of varieties are available (photo, above).

For more on all these readily available Bearded Irises, see Chapter 2.

Aril Irises

A quite distinct kind of bearded irises, not so readily available and harder to grow, is distinguished from the ones already listed by an unusual seed. While the seeds of ordinary bearded irises are unremarkable, wrinkled brown affairs, these other bearded kinds have a more decorative seed. At one end of each seed is a white or creamy appendage called an **aril.**

Botanists have discovered that arils are often rich in sugars and oils. These little food packets are very attractive to ants. After the seeds have fallen from the pods, ants pick them up and carry them off to eat the arils. Having done that, they find the hard coat of the seed itself too difficult to deal with, and drop it. In this way the seeds are dispersed far and wide, allowing the plants to take hold in new areas.

Collectively, these irises are called **Arils,** after the seed appendage, and the grouping includes Oncocyclus and Regelia Irises (discussed on the facing page), among others. Many Aril Irises make their homes in the deserts of the Middle East and north into the Caucasus Mountains, and others are found in Afghanistan and

Mongolia. Away from their native habitats, they may be a challenge to grow unless conditions are similar to their home ground.

Oncocyclus Irises, or Oncos, are true desert dwellers. Their buried, gnarled rhizomes send up curved, sickle-shaped leaves and stout stems that bear just a single flower (photo, below left). But what flowers! Some of them are truly enormous, as much as 8 in. in diameter, and they may have unusual color combinations, with large contrasting spots (called signals) beneath the beards and intricate patterns of veins and dots.

Close cousins to the Oncos, **Regelias** (sometimes called **Hexapogons**) have elegant, silky flowers (photo, below right) with beards on both standards and falls. They are not so highly adapted to deserts, and have been found in mountain valleys over a large part of southwestern and central Asia. Their rhizomes often send out long, thin runners so that new plants emerge some distance from the parent. The exotic blooms are smaller than those of the oncos and are carried two to a stem.

Regelias combine elegant, tapered form and unusual colors, as shown by the species *Iris stolonifera* (above).

The hybrid Oncocyclus Iris 'Emek' (left), blooming in production fields in Israel.

Crossing Arils with bearded irises produces Arilbreds, which are easier to grow than their pure Aril ancestors.

Dutch plant breeders found that Oncos and Regelias would cross rather easily, and they produced a series of beautiful (and more easily grown) hybrids called **Regeliocyclus** Irises. All three of these Aril types can be crossed with "ordinary" Bearded Irises, and the resulting varieties are called **Arilbreds** (photo, above), many of which can be grown in home gardens. For more about Arils and their hybrids, see Chapter 7.

BEARDLESS IRISES

Beardless irises differ from bearded ones in having smooth falls and smaller, more fibrous rhizomes. Beardless irises also have a much wider variety of flower and plant forms: If it can be believed, they are even more diverse than their bearded cousins. Many of them thrive where bearded irises do not, as along the Gulf Coast of the United States, while others are among the hardiest of all irises. There are beardless irises for every garden and nearly every situation. Here they are discussed roughly in the order of their need for water, starting with the least thirsty.

Spuria Irises

The **Spurias** come from southern Europe, Russia, Turkey, Iran, and Iraq. A typical hybrid Spuria Iris is quite tall—up to 5 ft. in bloom—with vigorous strappy foliage that grows from a completely buried rhizome (top photo, facing page).

Spurias are particularly valuable in helping prolong the iris season, usually coming into their own just after the Tall Bearded Irises have finished blooming. The flowers come in nearly all colors save true red and resemble much larger versions of the florist's Dutch Irises. They're carried on stems with branches held very close to the main stalk, giving the appearance of a spike of flowers.

Although some varieties stay green and grow on through the summer, most are summer dormant and even lose their leaves in hot weather. Efforts are underway to produce Spurias that will do well in the eastern part of North America, and already considerable success has been achieved. But because so many are best adapted to climates with hot, dry summers, they will be dealt with in Chapter 7, which covers irises for drier environments.

Siberian Irises

Undoubtedly the best known and most widely grown beardless irises are the **Siberian Irises** (photo, below right). Siberians are known for their slender, graceful stems and foliage, both of which spring from finger-size, somewhat furry-looking rhizomes. Stems are generally about 2 ft. to 4 ft. tall, often branched, and carry flowers from 2 in. to 6 in. in diameter.

This set has two subdivisions: True Siberians and Sino-Siberians. The true Siberians are native to Europe, eastern Russia, China, and Japan. They are technically distinguished because they have 28 chromosomes in each of their cells (the subject of chromosome numbers is discussed in the sidebar on pp. 34-35). The true Siberians are widely adaptable meadow plants, which makes them ideal for incorporation in mixed borders. Their flowers come in shades of purple, blue, wine, and pink, and a few yellows have just been developed. Sino-Siberian Irises (they have 40 chromosomes) are found in the mountains of western China, and while beautiful in their own way are less adaptable; they require cool summers and a constant supply of moisture. The Siberians and Sino-Siberians are discussed in Chapter 3.

Pacific Coast Native Irises

Closely related to the Sino-Siberians are the **Pacific Coast Native Irises,** a grouping made up of a number of species and natural hybrids native to Oregon and California. Low-growing and exceptionally colorful (top photo, p. 18), PCNs (as their friends call them) are

Tall, striking Spuria Irises thrive where summers are dry. They blend well with Asiatic hybrid lilies.

Siberian Irises are the ideal border perennial.

Pacific Coast Native Irises are an excellent choice for West Coast gardens, but a challenge to grow elsewhere. Nevertheless, this clump of *Iris douglasiana* is thriving in a northern Virginia garden.

unfortunately not easy to grow away from their home environments; they need mild winters and dry summers. Where conditions are similar to their Pacific Coast home, however, as in parts of Britain, New Zealand, and Australia, PCNs thrive and are extremely popular.

Pacific Coast Native Irises cross easily with Sino-Siberians, providing a series of lovely hybrids called **Calsibes.** Look for more information on PCNs and Calsibes in Chapter 8.

Louisiana Irises

The popularity of **Louisiana Irises** has been gaining momentum in recent years, and with good reason. Even though the hybrid Louisianas, of which there are already hundreds of varieties, are based on species native to the Gulf Coast, Lower Mississippi Valley, and from Florida to South Carolina, they have proven to be hardy in New England and the northern Midwest. And, despite their origins as swamp dwellers, they can be perfectly happy away from water.

From 1 ft. to 4 ft. tall, these plants have flowers that can be as much as 7 in. across. Louisianas have a wider color range than any other kind of iris (photo, bottom left), including Tall Bearded Irises, since Louisianas feature true reds, a color yet to be attained in the bearded hybrids. Rhizomes are large, yam-like and profusely branching. These up-and-coming Americans get a detailed treatment in Chapter 4.

Japanese Irises

Japanese Irises love moisture. Like Louisianas, Japanese Irises have big, spectacular flowers (photo, facing page) and seem just as happy with moderate, but constant, supplies of

Louisiana Irises, bred from American natives, have the widest color range of any group of irises.

Four hundred years of selection have produced many hundreds of varieties of Japanese Irises. Even plants grown from random seed may be garden-worthy, as shown by these seedlings in the author's garden.

moisture as they do near bogs or ponds. As a bonus, they are the latest-blooming of the major iris groups, carrying the season on into August in the northern parts of the United States.

The most striking Japanese Irises are called "doubles," although what has really happened is that the standards have been replaced by another set of falls, producing a flat flower as much as 8 in. across. The color range resembles that of the Siberians, but real diversity comes in an astonishing array of patterns. The 3-ft. to 4-ft. bloomstalks are produced among narrow leaves from surprisingly small rhizomes.

At first selected for several centuries by Japanese devotees, then intensively bred for a few more, Japanese Irises are enjoying a renaissance in the hands of American breeders. You can read more about these showy flowers in Chapter 6.

The Laevigata group

The **Laevigatas,** another grouping of wetland species, include Asian, North American, and European natives. They're usually found in the wild in standing water, but gardeners have experimented with them and found that if well watered, they can be grown under drier conditions.

The Asian arm of this tribe is represented by *Iris laevigata* itself, a delightful iris from which the Japanese have selected a large number of varieties. Blues, purples, and whites dominate, often with unique dappled or spattered patterns. From North America come the native Blue Flag *(Iris versicolor)* and the Virginia Iris *(Iris virginica).* Their flowers remind one of those of Siberian Irises, though there are many more per stem. *I. versicolor* (top photo, p. 20) presents a wide variety of color forms. Breeders in several parts of the world have found that these three species *(laevigata, versicolor,* and *virginica)* can be interbred, and

Iris versicolor, **the Blue Flag, is found in wetlands throughout northeastern North America. As its Latin name suggests, flower color is highly variable.**

Iris pseudacorus **is a Eurasian native now widely established in North American ponds and marshes.**

we can expect a whole new race of beardless iris hybrids from their work.

While shades of blue and violet dominate in the Laevigata group, yellow is introduced by means of the European native *I. pseudacorus,* an adaptable plant that has colonized much of eastern North America (photo, below). *Iris setosa,* found in North America and northwestern Asia, is peculiar for having no standards (pardon the pun). It is easily grown. *Iris setosa*, technically in another group, can be crossed not only with Laevigatas, but with Siberian Irises as well. Find out more about these moisture-loving irises in Chapter 6.

CRESTED IRISES

We've talked of bearded and beardless irises, but here's a group that fits in neither category. Their falls are not smooth, but instead of a beard, there is a narrow crest of small, fleshy, finger-like projections (photo, below left). It's a small collection of species, but includes the only really tropical irises, along with some very hardy woodlanders like the diminutive North American native, *Iris cristata* (photo, below right). *Iris tectorum*, the Chinese Roof Iris, is another Crested Iris. You can read more about these plants in Chapter 8.

BULBOUS IRISES

The distinction between rhizomes and bulbs has already been explained (see pp. 8-10). Irises that grow from bulbs have never quite attained the garden popularity of the rhizomatous kinds, and this is a shame. They include some exceptionally beautiful, inexpensive, and easy-to-grow plants. Let's look at them briefly, in the order in which they flower. For more on irises from bulbs, see Chapter 5.

The crest of a Crested Iris is made up of fleshy projections from the fall petals. Shown above is *Iris tectorum album*.

Iris cristata, **shown at right, is a woodland species from the Appalachian Mountains. It is only a few inches tall.**

The dwarf bulbous *Iris reticulata* blooms with crocuses.

Reticulata Irises

The first bulbous irises to bloom are the **Reticulatas,** which can appear even in late winter, and share the early stage with species crocuses. They are small, in the crocus size range, with flowers up to 2 in. or 3 in. in diameter carried only a few inches above the soil (photo, left). Reticulatas are frequently strongly scented. The leaves, rush-like in appearance, may later grow more than 1 ft. tall, but at flowering time, they are scarcely taller than the blooms themselves.

The name of the group comes from the distinctive netted (reticulate) outer coat of the bulbs. Blue and violet *Iris reticulata* and *I. histrioides* are readily available and often very

A mass planting of Dutch Irises can be highly colorful.

cheap; the yellow *I. danfordiae* is harder to find. Just recently, numbers of newer hybrids, such as the yellow-and-blue 'Katherine Hodgkin', have appeared on the retail bulb market. That suggests that popularity might be on the way for these miniatures.

Xiphiums: Dutch, Spanish and English Irises

The florist's irises are the **Dutch hybrids** (bottom photo, facing page). Bred from species found mostly in Spain, Portugal, and Morocco, many millions of these are raised each year; the bulbs are discarded after they produce flowers for cutting and shipment. According to one authority, only about 5% of the bulbs are sold to gardeners. However, these bulbs are so inexpensive (especially when bought in quantity) and so easy to grow that they deserve more attention. Commercially, less than a dozen varieties are readily available, most of them with clear, single colors in blue, yellow, white, and violet. Less known are other kinds (like the 'Beauty' series) with complex, fascinating combinations of these colors in the same flower.

Closely related to the Dutch hybrids are the so-called **Spanish Irises,** which have smaller flowers, more like the wild species. Available only as mixtures, they are often dominated by yellow and bronze varieties. Both of these types thrive best in regions with hot, dry summers, but can be grown almost as annuals in less favorable climates.

Little known in North America are the **English Irises,** which are not English at all but bred from the species *Iris latifolium,* a native of moist meadows in the high Pyrenees of Spain and France. These irises bloom later than the Dutch and Spanish varieties, with larger flowers. You can get them in shades of blue and violet, as well as pristine white. Unlike their Dutch and Spanish cousins, they do best where summers are cool and moist.

Juno Irises

As many as one-third of all named *Iris* species belong to the bulbous group known as **Junos,** but of these no more than three or four are used by gardeners. Junos are so different in all respects from other irises that some authorities consider them to belong to their own genus, called *Juno* or sometimes *Scorpiris.* These irises grow from a bulb that also produces thickened, daylily-like roots. The most commonly grown garden species, *Iris bucharica,* looks like a miniature corn plant 8 in. to 12 in. tall, with large yellow and white flowers carried in the axils of the leaves, where one would expect the ears of corn to be (photo, below). With the exception of this species and a few others, growing in pots may be the best way to handle Junos, which require a summer dormant period.

***Iris bucharica* is the only one of many Juno Iris species that is readily available to home gardeners.**

BEARDED IRISES

The gardener who first becomes interested in irises and requests a color catalog from one of the major growers of Tall Bearded Irises will be stunned by the sheer numbers of patterns, colors, and forms in this plant grouping. It's easy to see how thousands of American gardeners have come to specialize in this single kind of iris, with some collections holding several hundred varieties or even moving into subspecialties defined by stature, color, or pattern.

Paging through your first iris catalog can be inspirational, but it can also be confusing. In the plant descriptions, you'll encounter unfamiliar terms, most of which refer to the forms and patterns of iris flowers. This chapter will provide some guidance. Then we'll move on to the genesis of modern Tall Bearded Iris hybrids. Finally, the bulk of this chapter will tell you how to grow them.

Pattern, Color, and Form

We talked briefly of the parts of an iris flower on pp. 6-7, but terms such as standards and falls are just the beginning of the language of irises. There are many more terms to learn, and most of these refer to pattern, color, and form. To make sure you plant varieties with the characteristics you want in your garden, it helps to be comfortable with the lingo.

PATTERN

Perhaps the most frequently used term to describe color pattern in irises is **self.** An iris described as a self is one that is entirely, or almost entirely, one color; for example, a blue self should have standards and falls of exactly the same shade of blue (photo, below left). The color of the beard may also be the same, or it may be contrasting—the most popular pink irises have beards of a much richer, deep tangerine-orange color, and some breeders have succeeded in moving these reddish beards even to white and blue selfs.

If the standards are of a lighter shade than the falls, the iris is called a **bitone** (photo, below center). Reverse bitones have lately appeared as well, with the standards darker than the falls. **Bicolors** have the standards and falls of two distinctly different colors; for example, the standards may be violet or purple and the falls orange, red, or bronze (photo, below right).

'Silverado', the 1994 Dykes Medal winner, is an excellent example of a light-blue self.

In a bitone iris, the standards are a lighter shade of the same color as the falls. 'Rustler' also shows exuberant ruffling of all petals.

Bicolors, such as 1993 Dykes Medal winner 'Edith Wolford', have standards and falls of entirely different colors.

A variegata is a special class of bicolor with yellow standards and red or red-purple falls. Shown above is 'Gypsy Caravan'.

White standards over colored falls mark an amoena. 'Bright Hour' (right) is a classic that has been in gardens for many decades.

With color applied to the edges of white or yellow petals, plicatas present a brilliant show. 'Jesse's Song' (far left) won its Dykes Medal in 1990.

Luminatas such as 'Mind Reader' (left) come from plicata breeding but have a more subtle pattern.

Some bicolors have their own special names (photos, facing page). A bicolor iris with yellow standards and red or purple falls is called a **variegata** (this color pattern is inherited from one of the ancestral species, *Iris variegata*). If the standards are white and the falls purple, the iris is an **amoena** (a Latin word meaning "pleasant"). There are also amoenas with falls of yellow, pink, red, and blue.

There are also terms that describe the ways in which colors are applied to the petals. A **plicata** has a white or light-yellow ground color with darker markings of red, blue, or violet applied around the edge of each petal (photo, above left). The markings often look like stitching, since the color concentrates at the ends of the petal's veins. In many plicatas, the darker color is so generously supplied that the standards show little if any of the ground color, which

appears only as a spot on the falls below the beard. A fairly recent development is the combination of the plicata pattern with variegata and amoena types: the plicata pattern appears only on the falls, and the standards are clear white or yellow. **Luminatas** are an offshoot of plicata breeding, though they look quite different. In this pattern (photo, above right), the white ground appears brushed with color, interrupted by white veins.

COLOR AND TEXTURE

Tall Bearded Irises come in a virtually endless range of colors. There is every conceivable shade of blue and violet, ranging from an icy white to deep tones indistinguishable from black. Yellows go from lemon-tinted whites through golds and apricots to deep oranges, often with fiery red beards. Developed mostly from yellow progenitors, pink irises in shades from deep tangerine to pale buffy-pink may also carry startling red beards. While no true spectrum red has appeared (that pigment may be missing from the genetic palette of the TBs), near-reds, coppery browns, and brown-blacks are known.

The texture of the petals may be glossy and finished, velvety and plush-like, or anything in between. A few "diamond-dusted" varieties actually sparkle in the sunlight; their petals carry scattered groups of cells that reflect light.

THE EVOLUTION OF FORM

Historically, flower form has changed a great deal under the hand of the modern breeder. This revolution in form began with the TBs and has moved into all of the other classes. The breeding material with which hybridizers began at the turn of the 20th century had relatively small flowers with narrow petals. Standards often were imperfectly upright and tended to lean outward, while falls hung straight down and were narrow, sometimes pinched in at the sides.

For better or worse (and there is debate), all that has changed. The typical modern TB has very broad petals, up to 4 in. across, so that an individual flower more than 6 in. high has become the norm. The standards arch inward and support each other rather than collapsing outward; the falls nearly always have some degree of flare, ranging up to the horizontal, and are so wide that their hafts touch each other. With more petal surface available to display color, the impact of these modern varieties in the garden is many times that of the "ancients."

Ruffles and lace

Along with changes in flower form, breeders have also developed a wide range of petal edgings. The smoothly tailored petal edge of the older varieties is still treasured, but most modern kinds show some degree of ruffling, caused by the more rapid growth of the petal margins, and this adds a pleasing informality. Laced edges are also found; the petals of these irises are finely frilled and crimped (photo at left, facing page). When lacing and ruffling are combined it can be little too much!

Horns and flounces

About 50 years ago, a new characteristic appeared in Tall Bearded Irises that became the focus of attention of a number of hybridizers. It had been noticed that a few iris seedlings had a small, fleshy extension at the tip of the beard, so that the outer part of the beard was raised above the surface of the fall. With selection, this genetic change was accentuated so that nearly the whole beard occupied a distinct, upturned horn (photo at right, facing page). 'Unicorn', the first of these varieties to be named and introduced, was bred by Lloyd Austin, of Placerville, California. Later, the horn itself became broadened at the tip as a spoon-shaped extension, and finally as a "flounce," an almost petal-like structure.

Now called "Space Age" irises, these unusual forms were at first controversial and the focus of only a small group of avid collectors. Now, more than four decades after the introduction

'Laced Cotton' (far left) exhibits heavy lacing of the petal edges.

"Space Age" bearded irises have a petal-like extension at the tip of the beard. The variety shown at left is 'Sky Hooks', an important parent for this trait.

of 'Unicorn' in 1954, "Space Agers" have penetrated the general iris market, and are being listed by the major growers. 'Thornbird', the 1997 Dykes Medal winner, is the first horned iris to win that top award.

Stem Height, Flower Size, and Time of Bloom

As you thumb through iris catalogs and try to winnow down your choices, you will undoubtedly factor in the height of the stem, the size of the flower, and the timing of bloom. Because modern bearded irises have been raised from species ranging from just a few inches to

over a yard tall, with flowers of corresponding sizes, a classification system based on stem height and flower size was set up some years ago by the American Iris Society (see the sidebar on pp. 30-31). Most catalogs use the nomenclature of this classification system.

WHAT LOOKS BEST WHERE

Irises can be better displayed if there is some variation in the height at which the blooms are placed. You will probably want to select both taller and shorter varieties. Each iris type has its own distinctive uses in the garden. The potential uses of the various types are, of course, suggested by their size.

Miniature Dwarfs (photo at left, p. 32) are wonderful rock-garden plants; they can also do well as parts of compositions in large troughs or containers. They are extremely hardy, but because of their small size are easily overwhelmed by aggressive plants near them, and they can be easily uprooted by over-enthusiastic weeding.

A good use for Standard Dwarfs is as a planting in front of a collection of taller bearded irises. They also do well in rock gardens or gardens designed to simulate a natural environment. When well grown, Standard Dwarfs create brilliant displays of sheets of color held several inches off the ground. They are very hardy, tough plants.

Intermediate varieties have the virtue of extending the Bearded Iris season on the early side. Because of their vigor, they are not likely to be lost when planted among the taller kinds. Intermediates do well in perennial borders if protected from encroaching neighbors; they bloom at a season when their wide color range is especially welcome.

THE CLASSIFICATION OF GARDEN BEARDED IRISES

The American Iris Society recognizes six groupings of bearded irises. Starting with the smallest, these are Miniature Dwarfs, Standard Dwarfs, Miniature Talls, Intermediates, Borders, and Talls (see the chart on the facing page).

Miniature Dwarfs must be less than 8 in. tall, with flowers 2 in. to 3 in. across on unbranched stems. They are derived from the southern European species, *Iris pumila*. Miniature dwarfs are the first bearded irises to bloom, often with the Dutch crocuses. The falls of these irises sometimes have curious "thumbprints" in a color that contrasts with the rest of the flower.

Standard Dwarfs are from 8 in. to 15 in. tall and carry 2-in. to 4-in. flowers on stems that are sometimes branched. They bloom after the Miniature Dwarfs, usually with daffodils and early tulips.

Intermediates have 3½-in. to 5-in. flowers on stems that are 16 in. to 27 in. tall, and at least one branch. They bloom later than the two dwarf categories, but before the usual Tall Bearded Irises—often at the same time as the late tulips, which they complement very nicely.

Border Bearded Irises are like the Intermediates in nearly every respect, though their flowers are sometimes slightly larger. They differ in blooming later, with the Tall Bearded Irises.

Miniature Tall Bearded Irises bloom with the regular Talls and Border Bearded Irises and have the same height range as the latter, but present a more delicate look. Their stems are thinner, and their flowers are smaller and more in proportion to the stalk height.

Tall Bearded Irises are taller than 27 in., with flowers 4 in. to 7 in. (or more) across. Catalog descriptions usually give a range of stem heights (generally from 28 in. to 48 in.). These are the last of the Bearded Irises to bloom.

Border Bearded Irises are suitable for border plantings—hence the name. They also make wonderful foreground plants in a collection of taller hybrids.

Miniature Talls, once called "Table Iris," are outstanding for cutting due to their moderate size, slender stems, and graceful flowers. Their refined appearance makes them ideal for flower arrangements, since they will not overpower other elements.

Tall Bearded Irises are vastly popular. They look best in a setting either dedicated to them alone or in which they unquestionably dominate.

Therefore, companion plants must be chosen with an eye toward their compatibility with the irises.

A MATTER OF TIMING

Most individual iris varieties have a short blooming season, and many people think that's their biggest drawback. But it shouldn't discourage you from growing them. By planting a good range of types and varieties, it is possible to have bearded irises blooming continuously for up to three months!

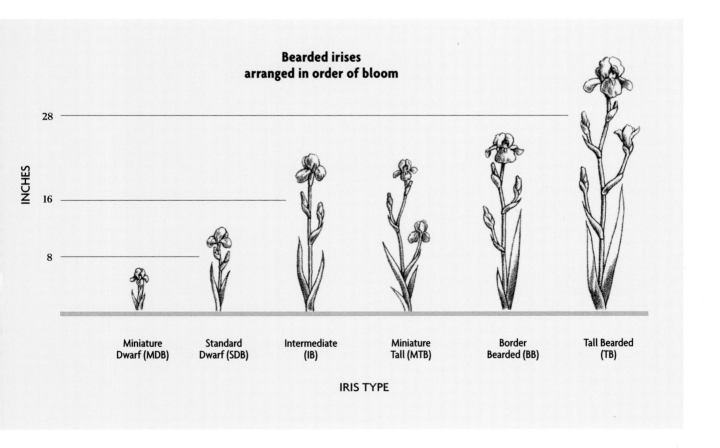

Bearded irises arranged in order of bloom

INCHES

28

16

8

| Miniature Dwarf (MDB) | Standard Dwarf (SDB) | Intermediate (IB) | Miniature Tall (MTB) | Border Bearded (BB) | Tall Bearded (TB) |

IRIS TYPE

Miniature Dwarf Bearded Irises make ideal rock-garden plants, as suggested by this picture of *Iris attica* (above) in its native habitat in Greece.

At right, Bearded Irises with compatible companion perennials.

In many Tall Bearded Iris catalogs, time of bloom is referred to as early, midseason, or late. The Tall Bearded Iris bloom season, from the earliest to the latest bloomers, is rarely more than four weeks. You need to decide if you want one grand midseason explosion, or a more sedate, prolonged period of iris enjoyment. If the information is available, a description of the branching habits of the varieties is very useful, since more branches mean more buds, and more buds mean a longer season for that variety.

Of course, the bearded iris season is not just that explosion of color provided by the Tall Bearded hybrids. Miniature and Standard Dwarfs begin early, following hard on the heels of the crocus and daffodil, while Intermediates bridge the gap to the talls. Summer and autumn bloom is now provided by reblooming Tall Bearded varieties (see the sidebar on the facing page); there are even a few Standard Dwarfs which, in the right climate, are continuous bloomers.

REBLOOMING BEARDED IRISES

The traditional blooming season for bearded irises is the late spring or early summer. But ever since irises were brought into gardens centuries ago, growers have sometimes been surprised by varieties reblooming in late summer, fall, or even early winter, if the climate is mild. This phenomenon seems particularly pronounced among the Intermediates, whose first blooming season is on the early side in any case. A few old kinds of Intermediates and Talls rebloom with some reliability if growing conditions are favorable.

The tendency to rebloom is hereditary; that is, seedlings from reblooming parents also rebloom. At the core of this genetic potential is evidently much faster, more vigorous growth than is normal, so that rebloomers mature blooming-size rhizomes in the late summer, rather than in the late fall. By selecting parents that have stronger and stronger reblooming tendencies, breeders have been able to create irises that will rebloom in most years, providing an exciting feeling of spring in autumn.

The future looks bright for reblooming (or remontant) irises, but only a part of their promise has been realized. Breeders have as their immediate goal varieties that are the equal of any "once bloomers" and that bloom reliably at least twice a year. But that's not all—meet with these enterprising hybridizers and they soon begin to talk about the possibility of continuous bloom in irises! Already there are a few Miniature and Standard Dwarf varieties that have the potential to bloom three times a year.

Right now, rebloom is something of a gamble that depends on the genetic potential of the iris, the gardener's cultural practices, and the climate. Given a very strong tendency to rebloom, a variety like Lloyd Zurbrigg's award-winning 'Immortality' needs the best of growing conditions, including watering during summer droughts and perhaps extra feeding. This carries some dangers, since the resulting growth may be soft and more susceptible to diseases and pests. Protection against debilitating diseases such as leaf spot (see pp. 51-52) is also a must.

Indeed, some varieties with strong reblooming potential seem less winter hardy than varieties that do not rebloom. Here is where climate plays a role. If mild weather persists long into winter, as in southern California, the chance for rebloom is enhanced because rhizomes have longer to mature, and emerging bloomstalks will not be cut down by frosts. In contrast, to get rebloom in New England, varieties must grow rapidly enough to be able to produce bloom in August or September. Some, surprisingly, are capable of doing just that.

Achieving rebloom in irises requires careful selection of varieties, the best possible care and culture, a relatively mild climate, and perhaps most important, good fortune. But if hybridizers have their way, the Tall Bearded Irises of the next century will have extended blooming seasons far beyond anything dreamed of just a few decades ago.

Almost everblooming in mild climates, the reblooming Standard Dwarf Bearded Iris 'Baby Blessed' brightens a late-summer border with dahlias and butterfly bushes.

Tolerance to Cold

There is one more consideration in selecting irises, and it's a practical one: Will the plant survive in your climate? In order to answer that question, we digress for a moment into history. In the late 19th century, after nearly 400 years of development as garden plants, Tall Bearded Irises had reached a dead end, with refinements slow in coming and minor in nature. Breeders had worked only with a small number of species native to central and southern Europe, all of which were diploids. By this we mean that each individual cell of each plant carried only two complete sets of chromosomes, and thus had limited potential for genetic combination (see the sidebar below for a more scientific explanation).

In the 1880s, plant explorers found tetraploid Bearded Iris species in the Middle East and western Asia. These plants, which carried four complete sets of chromosomes, had double the potential for genetic variation of the previously known forms. Quickly, iris breeders began to work with these species, and by the 1930s the

DIPLOIDS AND TETRAPLOIDS

Gardeners today are more scientifically savvy than gardeners of 20 years ago, but many are still baffled by the terms "diploid" and "tetraploid." These words should be a part of the gardener's vocabulary because they are being encountered more and more as plant breeders learn to manipulate heredity in surprising ways.

As most people know, all living things are made up of tiny units called cells. A single iris plant, for instance, contains billions of cells, and all of them are direct descendants of a single fertilized egg. At the core of each cell is a structure called the nucleus, which contains the genetic instructions necessary to operate the cell. Since all the cells in the plant are identical to each other and to the original fertilized egg, the nucleus likewise contains all of the genetic information required to determine the shape, color, size, and other characteristics of the plant.

The information is encoded on minute rod-like bodies called chromosomes. Microscopic examination shows that in all of the cells except those concerned directly with reproduction (pollen and ovules) there are actually two full sets of chromosomes, and thus two copies of each gene. This condition of having two sets of chromosomes in the nuclei is referred to by geneticists as diploidy, and plants of this kind are called **diploids.** In the natural world, virtually all plants (and animals) are diploid.

Among plants, by means too complex to explain briefly, the number of chromosome sets occasionally doubles (this almost never happens in animals), so that the cells of the plant contain four, not two, full sets of chromosomes. Such plants are **tetraploids.** Tetraploid plants do occur in nature, and a number of *Iris* species, such as *I. pumila, I. trojana, I. hoogiana,* and *I. mesopotamica* are naturally occurring tetraploid species. Tetra-ploidy can also be induced by treating parts of plants or plant embryos with the chemical colchicine, a deadly poison extracted from the bulbs of species of *Colchicum,* an autumn-flowering crocus relative. Most of the plants and embryos so treated die, but a few are converted to tetraploidy.

Tetraploid plants contain double the genetic information of diploids, and often are more vigorous and larger than their diploid counterparts. More significantly, they have four, rather than two, copies of each of their genes, transition from diploid to tetraploid hybrids was nearly complete. Today, diploid varieties are treasured and preserved primarily as historical reminders. Modern Tall Bearded hybrids are tetraploid, though nearly all of them carry genes from the old diploids.

What does all this have to do with tolerance to cold? If you recall the origins of the plants, the tetraploid forms, which came from relatively warm areas, were not reliably cold hardy and frequently failed to survive winters in western Europe and northern North America. The diploid forms, which came from Europe, were

of extraordinary toughness. All this is by way of saying that there is a considerable range of tolerance of cold and of summer humidity among modern Tall Bearded Iris hybrids. Those with genes mostly from the Middle Eastern tetraploids are sensitive to winter freezes and prolonged, warm, rainy summers, while those with genes from the older European varieties are better suited to places where such conditions occur.

which allows for more variation in such things as flower color and form. Thus the appearance of tetraploidy in a genus of garden plants, whether natural or induced, is cause for rejoicing. The event usually marks a new burst of hybridization and a spate of new, strongly improved varieties. The tetraploid revolution in Tall Bearded Irises began around the turn of the century, with the introduction of varieties based on naturally occurring tetraploids from Asia. Normally, tetraploids and diploids cannot be crossed successfully, but in hundreds of attempts, the occasional seed is produced, and if it can be successfully germinated, the resulting plant may also be a tetraploid. In this way, the genes of the diploids were introduced into tetraploid breeding lines.

Many hybridizers took up the challenge, and by 1925, nearly all new irises being introduced were tetraploids.

'Snow Flurry,' a tetraploid white, is perhaps the most important Tall Bearded Iris hybrid in history.

In the late 1930s, in San Jose, California, Clara Rees crossed 'Purissima', a white tetraploid, with 'Thais,' a pink diploid. The single resulting seed produced a tetraploid white, 'Snow Flurry', arguably the first modern iris. 'Snow Flurry' (photo, left), with its flaring form and broad, ruffled petals, was a true break-through. When nurseryman Carl Salbach saw the plant, he immediately bought up all the stock for introduction in 1939. 'Snow Flurry' is to be found in the ancestry of many popular iris varieties, and shortly after it came on the scene, diploids were abandoned completely. Smaller diploids have hung on, however, in the Miniature Tall Bearded class.

In other kinds of irises, the tetraploid revolution is yet to take place. Tetraploids have been induced in Siberian, Japanese and Louisiana Irises, but the vast majority of commercially available varieties are still diploids.

Buying Bearded Irises

Irises of various types are sold at discount stores, garden centers, and local general nurseries. The experience of most irisarians is that plants from these sources, while they may be healthy, vigorous and cheap, are very often mislabeled. When they bloom they may not match the picture on the box or the varietal name under which they were sold. To be sure of getting what you pay for, buy plants you have seen in bloom, or buy from a reliable vendor.

Irises are available from major mail-order houses, which have an interest in making sure their customers are well satisfied, and from specialist nurseries, which take particular care in providing their buyers with the best stock, accurately labeled. In my view, while an impulsive purchase once in while from a general supplier is all right, it's much better to buy irises from dealers who have grown the plants themselves and are specialists in irises. Here's why.

In North America, iris breeders take up residence wherever their favorite plant can be grown, and quite naturally, they select and name varieties that do well in their own gardens, not necessarily in yours. For example, iris varieties that are the product of a long breeding history in southern California may not perform up to expectations in Ohio or Virginia, and vice versa.

The bottom line? Buy your first plants from a nursery near you or from one that is located in the same climatic zone. This is not to say that irises from a grower in Oregon will not thrive in New England; most of them will. But if you are a beginner, why take a chance? Buy plants that you know are adapted to your own conditions. The best alternative is to visit the nursery and make your selection while the plants are in bloom.

Nurseries that specialize in irises range from backyard "mom and pop" operations to agribusiness establishments with hundreds of acres of irises and mechanized equipment for growing them. The latter produce beautiful, glossy color catalogs, while the former may have only a typed list. The color catalogs are mailed early in spring and they are worth having as references, even if you don't order from them. They cost from $2 to $5 each year, but in most cases the cost of the catalog can be deducted from your order. Lists from smaller gardens are often free or available for postage. On pp. 162-165 of this book, you'll find a list of over 100 gardens and nurseries that offer irises for sale. The list is arranged by state or province so you can easily find a supplier near you.

MAKING YOUR CHOICE

A recent count showed that over 27,000 bearded iris varieties have been registered by name, and probably about half of these are still in commerce. But most large iris nurseries (and even some smaller ones) offer about 200 to 400 varieties, ranging from the newest introductions to ones that were first brought to the market as much as 25 years before. A good number of iris nurseries specialize in "historic" varieties that were introduced before 1970. It goes without saying that a 25-year-old variety that is still being carried in catalogs has proven itself. And, of course, it will be far less expensive than the latest "improvement."

It's easy to go overboard with iris catalogs. Think carefully about the space and care requirements that are implied by the size of your order. My advice is to start with perhaps no more than a dozen or so carefully selected varieties, rather than to find yourself swamped with plants and out of time to care for them properly.

One way to be sure of getting the right varieties for you is to consult the American Iris Society, which has a regional organization; each region maintains lists of varieties that have been successful there. The AIS also conducts an annual national popularity poll; it is doubtful that a variety could make that list without being widely adaptable. American Iris Society major awards (such as the Dykes Medal, given to one outstanding variety each year) mark out vigorous, novel, widely adapted varieties. For more on the AIS, including top award winners from the past ten years and a recent popularity poll, see pp. 158-161.

PLACING YOUR ORDER

The best time to order irises through the mail is as soon after the catalogs arrive in spring as possible. Most growers fill orders in rotation, and some stocks may be exhausted late in the season. Shipping of Tall Bearded Irises begins as early as July, but you can specify when you want your plants shipped if you order early enough to allow the grower to plan. (Some growers ship beardless irises in either spring or fall, and bulbous irises are always shipped in fall along with other "Dutch" bulbs. After reading this book, you should know when to plant each type of iris in your region.)

COST

Prices for plants vary widely. Prices from big outfits that put out color catalogs tend to be high. Often the same variety, and the same-quality plant, can be had for as much as 50% less from a smaller operation. It pays to shop.

In 1997, prices for individual rhizomes of older iris varieties ranged from $4 to $6 each in the catalogs of the large growers. Smaller nurseries that do not annually produce expensive color catalogs may sell the same varieties for significantly less. New introductions may cost as much as $35 to $50. As more material of newer kinds is propagated, the price gradually goes down, and the introductions that stand the test of time become more affordable. Despite considerable hoopla from growers, many novelties sink beneath the waves in a few years and become hard to find. I think it's best to let this sorting-out process take its course before investing in an expensive new hybrid.

Nearly all iris growers offer collections of varieties at considerably reduced prices, and usually at least one of these collections will be labeled for beginners. While a collection may not give you the full range of choices you wanted, the cost will be far less than if the plants are bought separately. The varieties included will be old favorites that are very likely to succeed almost anywhere. I still remember with great pleasure the first blooming season of such a collection in my own garden, 40 years ago!

IRISES FOR FREE

Iris growers are proverbially generous. When your box of rhizomes arrives (sometime between July and September) it probably will contain not only what you ordered, but "extras," usually somewhat more expensive and recent varieties than the ones making up your order. Some mail-order iris nurseries specify the value of their extras and allow you to choose or suggest them. So, when you prepare your iris bed, always make ready somewhat more space than you think you need.

General Cultural Requirements

Although the focus of this section is on Tall Bearded Irises, the same general principles apply to all of the size classes of bearded irises. The smallest forms, such as the Miniature and Standard Dwarfs, enjoy the same kind of exposure and soil conditions as their larger relations, but often appreciate more meticulous attention to weeding, watering, and winter protection. Many of the smaller hybrids also multiply more rapidly than the Tall Bearded Irises, so more frequent replanting may be required, and many more new rhizomes will be produced. It should also be remembered that many Miniature and Standard Dwarfs require cold winters to set buds and bloom. They may not be at their best in more southerly regions (USDA Zone 8 and south).

Experienced gardeners know that plants do best when they are given the conditions under which they would thrive in the wild. Even though the TBs are many, many generations removed from their wild ancestors of Europe, the Middle East and western Asia, they still markedly prefer conditions that make them feel at home.

The wild bearded irises that are the progenitors of our hybrids are plants of open country. They grow where light and breezes are in generous supply, not smothered in undergrowth or deep in shady woods. In Europe, the remaining colonies of species are often to be found growing atop collapsed castle walls, on rocky crags, or on steep slopes. This speaks to a requirement for excellent drainage—no bogs or standing water.

The soils these wild irises favor are loamy and moderately supplied with nutrients. These soils are often derived from limestone, so they have an alkaline (or "sweet") nature and are rich in calcium. Few irises would do well in heavy clay.

Depending on where they live, the foliage may be nearly evergreen, may disappear completely in winter, or may languish in summer humidity. A tendency to grow in winter is characteristic of the less hardy species.

Given this information, a number of conclusions can be drawn. Iris plantings should be located in a sunny place, probably with a minimum of six hours of full sun each day. Experience has shown that the amount of bloom produced is directly related to the amount of sunlight the plants get—the more sun, the more bloom.

Good air circulation is essential. Without it, foliage diseases and rhizome rots thrive. Tall Bearded Irises do not respond well to crowding, and unfortunately this makes them less than ideal plants for a mixed border unless you can prevent their neighbors from encroaching on them.

Low spots in the garden are not the places to site bearded irises, while raised beds are ideal. Clay soils should be lightened with the addition of organic material such as compost or leaf mold, and the same treatment can add body to sandy soils. The pH of the soil should be tested and adjusted to neutral or somewhat alkaline, as described on p. 40.

Establishing an Iris Bed

Sun, soil, and drainage are the three essentials for growing healthy, vigorous Tall Bearded Irises. Under favorable conditions, your irises will naturally be more resistant to pests and diseases—keep them happy, and you'll be happy, too.

SELECTING THE SITE

If you buy from a catalog, your order of rhizomes will typically arrive in late July or early August. It is wise to start preparing the bed at least a month beforehand, so that the soil will have a chance to settle and any soil amendments will be thoroughly incorporated. Perhaps the most important thing about this month-long mellowing period is that it allows a healthy population of beneficial soil microorganisms to become established. It is primarily these microorganisms, and not materials weathering from soil particles, that will provide most of the nutrition for your plants.

Begin by selecting a sunny site that has good air circulation. Avoid low spots. If good drainage is not natural to the site, plan to make a raised bed. How much space do you need? That depends on how often you want to divide and replant your irises. Single rhizomes can be planted as close as 18 in. apart, but within two years they will be very crowded. Most experienced iris hobbyists recommend at least 4 sq. ft. (2 ft. by 2 ft.) per rhizome, which will allow three to four years of growth before substantial clumps will form and the irises will be ready for division and replanting.

Since I usually don't buy very expensive, recently introduced varieties, I can afford to plant at least three rhizomes of each. A small group makes a much more immediate impact than a single rhizome and lessens the chances of losing that variety completely to attack by pests or disease. On pp. 42-43 I'll describe my planting method for groups of three rhizomes of a single variety.

Of course the smaller forms of bearded irises can be planted much more closely. In my garden, for example, some clumps of Miniature Dwarfs haven't been moved for seven years or more. They are slowly expanding into the original space allotted them.

GETTING RID OF GRASS AND WEEDS

If the site for the bed is covered with lawn grass, turn over the sod with a spade or thoroughly incorporate it into the soil with a tiller. As the sod decays, it will enrich the soil. I'm firmly against using herbicides to eliminate grass before bed preparation; these substances have no place in the home garden.

If time permits, another way to get rid of the grass is by **solarization.** This method of bed preparation works best in sunny climates, and a full treatment takes two to three weeks. After marking out the size and shape of your iris bed, cover the area with clear plastic, held down at the edges by soil or rocks. The plastic will trap the sun's heat close to the soil, killing grass, weeds and their seeds, disease organisms, and pests. Please note that black plastic, often used by landscapers under mulch, will not work—it simply blocks the sun and does not produce the cooking effect needed.

Regardless of your early steps in bed preparation, deep tilling or digging is recommended. Loosen the soil at least 1 ft. down. Iris roots penetrate deeply, and their task will be easier if the soil is deeply prepared. Repeated raking, tilling, and pulling will eliminate weeds and stray grass plants over the subsequent weeks.

AMENDING THE SOIL

Take a sample of the soil from your site to your local cooperative extension agent for analysis. This will guide you in what you may need to add to the soil, but pay particular attention to the acid/alkaline balance (pH value). If the soil pH is below 7.0, lime will be needed to make it neutral or slightly alkaline. Use slaked lime for a quick reaction, or pelleted ground limestone for a slower, steadier change. If it can be found, **dolomitic** limestone, which contains additional magnesium, is preferable. Lime should be spread out over the surface and tilled in thoroughly, then the bed should be watered deeply.

The only other commercially available soil amendment I usually recommend is colloidal phosphate (ground phosphate rock), and this should be used only if a soil analysis shows a deficiency of phosphate. Of the "big three" plant nutrients (nitrogen, phosphate, and potash), phosphate is most important to successful bearded iris culture. Phosphate is the nutrient most quickly depleted by the vigorous growth of irises, and this may help to explain why irises will do particularly well in soils where they have never grown before.

Nitrogen is definitely detrimental to irises if applied with too liberal a hand. Excess nitrogen leads to soft, lush growth that is highly susceptible to disease, and it can suppress blooming as well. A good, organic-based soil with dense populations of microorganisms and earthworms will contain more than enough nitrogen to satisfy irises. Potash is usually sufficiently abundant for irises in most soils.

THE IMPORTANCE OF COMPOST

More and more gardeners are realizing that the health of the soil determines the health of their plants. The measure of a healthy soil lies in its populations of beneficial soil organisms, and these are supported in the soil by two main factors. First, the soil must have a loose enough texture to be well aerated, so that soil organisms can obtain oxygen, and second, these organisms need abundant food.

Food for soil organisms does not come from a bag but is nothing more than naturally occurring organic matter, preferably in the form of well-seasoned compost. Compost improves the conditions soil organisms need (by breaking up the soil and loosening its texture) and also provides the food they require. Once established and well fed, these microbes will extract nitrogen from the air and slowly and evenly release phosphate and potash from the decay of organic material.

Compost does this best because it already contains enormous populations of beneficial microbes. If animal manure is used, it must be well rotted (at least for a year outside); otherwise it will provide an excess of nitrogen, which leads to soft growth in irises and increased vulnerability to disease. Don't use ground bark or fresh sawdust—both lack nitrogen and usually lower the pH of the soil. Well-rotted sawdust and bark are excellent. Leaf mold (my personal favorite), which is produced by composting autumn leaves for a year or more, is also good, especially if it still retains a "chunky" texture.

Spread 4 in. to 6 in. of compost on the surface of the bed, and dig it in deeply. The deeper you mix the compost, the better—remember, some iris roots go deep while others explore the shallower layers of the soil. Over the month or so that the bed is allowed to mellow, it should be occasionally tilled and raked, to continue the mixing process. This period can also be used to plan your planting.

WHAT TO DO WHEN YOUR PLANTS ARRIVE

Your iris rhizomes will arrive packed loosely in shredded paper or wood excelsior in a cardboard container (top photo, below), usually with some ventilation holes in the sides. Keeping in mind the need for good air circulation, unpack the box immediately and spread out the rhizomes in a dry, shady place. They need not be planted immediately, since they will be in a dormant state, only to revive

Iris shipments should be unpacked when they arrive (top). Above, a healthy, well-cured commercial division of a Tall Bearded Iris, trimmed in the traditional manner.

when the roots come in contact with soil and water. If you can get them into the ground within a week, they should be just fine.

A good commercial division will have a large, solid rhizome without any signs of mold or decay (bottom photo, p. 41). The leaves will be trimmed to the traditional triangular shape, and about two-thirds the length of the roots will have been clipped. Tags with varietal names may be attached, or the name may be written on the leaf fan with a marker. (Hint: if the leaf on which the name has been written has dried out and the name can no longer be read, soak the leaf in a dish of water containing a little detergent. It will soon expand and flatten out, and the name will become legible.)

Have on hand a list of the varieties you ordered, with their colors, patterns, and stem heights. If the bed is to be viewed from one side, the taller varieties should be in the back if the bed; if it is to be viewed from all sides, put the taller ones

in the center. As for color, everyone has favorite combinations and schemes, so use your own taste. However, it's probably a good idea not to place varieties of a similar color right next to one another. The direct comparison may lessen the impact of both kinds.

PLANTING THE RHIZOMES

How the rhizome "faces" is also an important consideration. The fan of leaves emerges from one end of the rhizome, and as the clump develops it will tend to expand in this direction. If two rhizomes are planted so that their leaf fans point toward one another, they will soon close the gap, become crowded and perhaps even inextricably mingled.

As I've already mentioned, many experienced gardeners will allocate up to 4 sq. ft. for a single iris rhizome, planting it at least 24 in. from its neighbors. In the normal course of events, such a plant will develop into a large clump and not need dividing and replanting for at least three and possibly as many as five years. However, a more immediate show is produced by planting three or more rhizomes of the same variety in about the same amount of space. The trade-off is that you will certainly have to replant after three years.

I find it useful to outline the space allocated to each group of rhizomes with a little sprinkling of lime, forming a triangle about 20 in. to 24 in. on a side. Three rhizomes of a single variety are then arranged within each angle, with two of them facing outward and one toward the center of the triangle. The next group is set up in a complementary triangle, arranged opposite to the first (photo, left). This way of planting will

A planting area for three rhizomes of the same variety is outlined in lime (left), and the rhizomes are arranged to allow room for growth. In adjacent varieties (right), planting triangles are reversed.

PLANTING IRIS RHIZOMES

1. **Build up a small mound of soil in the center of the planting hole.**

2. **Center the rhizome on the soil mound and spread out the roots on either side.**

3. **Firm the soil around the roots. Newly planted rhizomes should be watered thoroughly.**

give a fuller effect in the garden from the first year onward. As the rhizomes branch out and increase, the spaces will fill in.

The planting hole should be about 8 in. to 10 in. deep, and of similar diameter. Use some of the excavated soil to build a mound in the center of the hole and place the rhizome on this hill, with the roots spread outward and down on all sides. How deep should the rhizome be set? That depends. In light-textured soils, it can be covered by as much as 1 in. of soil, but for average to heavier soils, the top of the rhizome is best left exposed to the healthful influences of sun and air. Remember that the rhizome is a stem, not a root, and needs to breathe! Rhizomes planted too deeply in heavy soil will also be more susceptible to rot. Be sure to firm the soil you replace in the planting hole. Ideally,

the rhizome should be at the crest of a small rise, with a gentle slope going down in all directions around it. The photos above show the sequence of events.

After all your plants are set, water thoroughly. Unless rains fail, no additional watering should be needed, but in areas of the country where evaporation is high and summer rains rare, about 1 in. of water a week will help the irises get established. Within about two weeks, branch roots will have grown out to anchor the transplanted rhizome, and some new leaf growth may be emerging from the center of the fan—both good signs. As new leaves continue to emerge, those at the outside of the fan will wither and turn brown. Periodially check their attachment to the rhizome, and as they loosen, pull them off and burn them. A number of iris diseases and pests winter over on old dead leaves.

CARE FOR THE FIRST YEAR

As the weather cools in the fall and frosts approach, you may want to think about a winter mulch for the newly planted irises. Many new plantings come through their first winter perfectly fine without any protection, but a number of experienced growers swear by the provision of some kind of winter mulch for the first year. In areas where there is a reliable, heavy snow cover that comes early and stays late, the snow will provide adequate protection.

Most Tall Bearded Irises are quite hardy, so the mulch is not really supposed to protect them against freezing. In fact, we want the ground to freeze and stay that way! Most winter damage to new plantings comes about as a result of freeze/thaw cycling that shoves the rhizomes out of the ground and makes them vulnerable to drying winds, sunburn, and sudden drops in temperature. So if you choose to mulch the first winter, wait until the ground has frozen.

If you do apply a mulch, it must be loose and airy, so it won't pack down and get soggy—a sure ticket to rotting rhizomes in the spring. Evergreen boughs and pine straw are good choices; don't use leaves, sawdust, or ground bark. When the weather has reliably warmed in the spring, remove the mulch thoroughly and carefully. Soon after, your new irises will begin to send up fresh, new leaves. As you did the previous summer and fall, monitor the older leaves carefully and pull them off to be burned when they have shriveled.

If your soil was well prepared, no fertilization will be required during the first year, but some people like to sprinkle a phosphate-rich organic source, such as rock phosphate, around the plants when they are about 6 in. high. Fertilization with high-nitrogen chemical preparations, such as lawn fertilizer, is not a good idea for irises.

Recently, some iris hobbyists have become enthusiastic about the use of ordinary alfalfa pellets (the kind used to feed horses or rabbits) on irises. In spring, the dry pellets are scattered lightly about the iris beds and disintegrate after the first few rains. As they decay, phosphate and nitrogen are released, but the major effect seems to be due to a hormone-like substance that promotes growth in a wide variety of plants, irises included.

As the bloom season approaches, fans that will produce flower stalks will become slightly swollen at the base, and soon the stems will emerge from their centers. Now comes one of the great experiences for a gardener—the breakfast (or pre-breakfast!) tour of the iris planting to see what new beauties are unfurling their petals each day. You will find that most modern Tall Bearded hybrids have very good lasting qualities; an individual flower will last for three to four days and will withstand even a stiff shower without much damage. But to my eye, there is something really unpleasant about a faded, sodden iris flower that is past its prime. So I take along a small bucket on these morning excursions and fill it with snapped-off, spent blossoms.

The blooming season will seem all too short (usually about three to four weeks for Tall Bearded Irises, if you have planted a good range of varieties). When it ends, you'll have a forest of tall green stalks to dispose of. On a bright, dry day, snap off each of these stalks and its spent fan close to the parent rhizome. Breaking can be done simply by grasping the stem close to the base and pushing it back away from the rhizome. Most, if not all, of the stalks will separate cleanly. Breaking is better than cutting because the break will occur between the plant cells, while a cut will pass through and damage many cells, allowing an entry for disease. The old stems should be disposed of, not composted, to avoid spreading disease. I bury mine under raised beds in the vegetable garden, where they quickly disappear.

During the rest of the year, established irises require little care except for attention to the signs of disease and the few iris pests (see pp. 49-57 for the various symptoms). Tall Bearded Irises are remarkably free of such troubles, and if problems do appear, they can be dealt with quickly and easily.

However, there are two things to avoid. Don't mulch bearded irises during the summer (it encourages rot), and don't cut off the leaves unless they begin to look really terrible. Somehow it has become folk wisdom to cut back iris leaves after blooming, but this only weakens the plants and steals flowers from next year's season.

Dividing and Replanting

When your iris clumps get crowded, it's time to divide and replant. Otherwise, the buildup of pests and disease organisms and the depletion of vital nutrients may weaken your plants, causing fewer rhizomes to reach blooming size each year. Tall Bearded Irises seem to thrive on frequent division and replanting, especially in fresh or newly reconditioned soil. In fact, the big rhizomes sent out by most growers are the product of annual division, and of growing in fields where crops other than irises have been planted for two or three years.

If you've followed the advice of the experts and given each newly set single plant about 4 sq. ft. of space, you're good for three to four years of enjoyment before the expanding clumps begin to approach each other, limiting air circulation and the rhizomes' access to the sun. If you've planted three rhizomes of a variety in a triangle, three years is really about the maximum time to leave them without division.

DIGGING UP AN OLD CLUMP

About a month to six weeks after blooming seems to be a good time to dig up and divide a clump. The plants are beginning to enter a summer period of partial dormancy, when leaf and root growth will slow down or cease. The objective is to divide and reset the plants before a second period of active root production occurs in late summer and fall.

This is one time when you do want to cut back the leaves, in order to balance the inevitable loss of roots when the plants are dug up. Do the leaf cutting before you dig up the clump; it makes the plants easier to handle. The clump can be easily uprooted with a spading fork and excess soil shaken off.

Examine the clump carefully. Only the large, healthy rhizomes from around the margins, with broad fans of leaves, should be considered for replanting. Old, spent rhizomes, while they may still be solid and have active roots, will not bloom again, and leaving them attached to the current year's rhizomes will do no good. But it is worth noting that some growers who want to increase their stock of a certain variety save these old rhizomes and plant them an inch or two deep in a propagation bed. Often they will produce some new offshoots that will reach salable size in a year or two.

Just as with old bloomstalks (see pp. 44-45), I think it's best to break off the rhizomes you want to save rather than cut them. These new divisions should be thoroughly washed with a hose and set to dry in an airy, shaded place, perhaps on sheets of newspaper or just lying on the grass. It's beneficial for the rhizomes to dry for several days, and since they are already largely dormant, no harm will be done. Their wounds will heal and callus, closing the door to bacteria and fungi. A few authorities even suspect that a thorough drying will cause more buds to be set for the next year.

After washing but before drying, give the leaves a final trim, to about 8 in. tall. Cutting to the traditional triangular shape will make it easier for new leaves to emerge from the center of the fan. If many long roots are present, cut off about two-thirds their length.

Unless you have a phenomenal memory, you should label each fan as you clean it, and it is probably best to deal with one variety at a time. You can use a spirit-based (not water-soluble) felt-tipped marker to write the varietal name directly on the fan. As the marked leaf withers, the writing will disappear.

RENEWING THE PLANTING BED

This is the time to add more compost and rock phosphate to your planting bed, as well as more lime or ground limestone if the pH has slipped toward the acid side. You can do this while the rhizomes are curing in the shade. The addition of 4 in. to 6 in. of compost, well-rotted sawdust, or leaf mold each time you replant will keep the soil microbes active and greatly reduce the need to supplement your plants' diet.

While bearded irises do best in soil where they have not been grown for some time, a complete change of scene is not often feasible for the home gardener. Thus the renewal of the soil in the bed is very important. A technique recommended by many iris growers that simulates a move to completely new soil is solarization (see p. 40). I'll go over it again here, because it is even more strongly recommended for soil in which irises have been growing for some time.

In this method, the soil for the bed is thoroughly tilled, and any amendments (compost, etc.) are added. Then the bed is covered with clear plastic sheeting, held down at the edges by rocks or shovelfuls of soil. Over the next few weeks, the sun will heat the soil under the plastic, destroying most of the disease-causing organisms and weed seeds it contains. The irises can then be planted in the solarized bed. Solarization works best in areas where a good deal of sunny weather can be counted on, and of course it requires at least two iris beds through which your plants must be rotated.

1.

2.

3.

4.

5.

DIVIDING AN OVERGROWN CLUMP

1. **An overcrowded clump of irises should be divided and replanted.**

2. **Cut back the leaves of irises to be replanted.**

3. **Use a spading fork to dig up the clump.**

4. **The old and new crisscrossing rhizomes in the clump form a tangled mass.**

5. **Break off healthy new rhizomes from the old clump.**

1.

2.

3.

4.

5.

REPLANTING

1. Give the leaves a final trim, angling upward to the center of the fan.

2. Trim off about two-thirds the length of the roots.

3. Don't rely on your memory; label the fans with a permanent felt-tipped marker.

4. A bucketful of compost will help renew the soil.

5. Replant the single divisions.

A NEW PLANTING PLAN

If you plan to use exactly the same amount of space to replant and not to break any new ground, it may be best to replant only one large rhizome of each variety, just as you did when you started. The benefit of this procedure is that three or four more years may pass before you need to work over the bed again. But if you do plant just one of each, you're taking the chance of losing that single rhizome and with it that variety from your collection. Also, for a while you'll miss out on the spectacular display you've gotten used to. For these reasons, most gardeners plant not one, but three or four of the best rhizomes of each variety, even though the planting may now have to be remade after just two years, or three at the most.

Using the triangular planting plan, three rhizomes should be planted as described on p. 42, with two fans facing outward (the fan of leaves on the outside of the triangle) and one facing inward, to fill in the center of the clump and present a balanced appearance. The triangles can be alternated, with the first having its base facing the edge of the bed, the second its point, the third its base, and so on. This arrangement makes the most efficient use of space.

In a four-rhizome planting plan, the three at the points of the triangle all point outward, and the fourth is planted in the triangle's center. This arrangement will result more quickly in an impressive display, but crowding will occur sooner, as well.

Water in the new planting thoroughly.

Now, if you turn back to the shady spot where you let the rhizomes dry, you'll undoubtedly see many excellent plants left over. These are to give away to your friends or to sell (cheap!) for the benefit of your favorite local charity. Members of iris societies, though, save their extras for trading and for a fund-raising auction.

Diseases

In order to become at all popular, any perennial plant on the market today has to be reasonably free of pests and diseases; gardeners just don't want to take the time to pamper plantings. Tall Bearded Irises fill the prescription as well as any other of the top five hobbyist's plants of the 1990s, but no plant is perfect. There are a few problems you have to watch out for. I'll discuss them here roughly in the seasonal order (spring to fall) in which you might spot them in a growing planting.

BACTERIAL SOFT ROT

As they age, old rhizomes that have bloomed out will gradually shrivel and disappear; this is a normal process that takes several years. Watch carefully, however, for signs of decay in healthy, growing divisions. Be especially keen to spot softness at the base of the leaf fan and toppling fans that have separated from the rhizome.

Bacterial soft rot is caused by a soil bacterium that can infect many root crops. Plant pathologists know it as *Erwinia carotovora* (Erwin's carrot-eater). Bacterial soft rot can be distinguished from other rhizome rots by the truly foul smell this bacterium produces. So if you notice mushy rhizomes, toppling leaf fans, and a disgusting odor, it's bacterial soft rot. This problem is not hard to deal with if it is caught early, when a rhizome is only partially decayed, but if not dealt with immediately, bacterial soft rot can destroy an entire clump in a few days.

The treatment is as follows: Use a sharpened teaspoon or a melon scoop to remove all rotted matter back to healthy, white, crisp tissue. If you're treating several rhizomes, dip your tool in a strong solution of chlorine laundry bleach (at least one part bleach to five parts water) between operations—bacteria can be spread by tools. Experience has taught that the best way to prevent the newly exposed, scraped surfaces from rotting anew is to dust them with a household cleanser that contains a chlorine-based bleach. This works three ways: It helps to dry the wound, the bleach is fatal to bacteria, and the cleanser produces a strong alkaline environment in which any surviving bacteria can't grow. There's no evidence that it hurts the irises. An alternative that also seems to work is agricultural sulfur dust.

Bacterial soft rot can be prevented by avoiding poorly drained sites and mulches and by replanting before serious crowding takes place. Do not add too much nitrogen, which can produce soft growth, inviting *Erwinia* to dine. The disease thrives in wet weather and is most problematic in the spring and late fall.

FUNGAL ROTS

Other serious rhizome rots are caused by infections of fungi that belong to a group which produces small, hard, spore-like bodies called sclerotia. The most commonly seen fungal rots are crown rot and botrytis rot. Because of the size and shape of their sclerotia, both villains are sometimes called mustard-seed fungi.

Fungal rots are difficult to deal with because the sclerotia can persist in the soil for long periods of time, giving rise to active infections when conditions favor them. The best preventive measures are cultural—making sure that your irises are not crowded, that the rhizomes enjoy good exposure to sunlight, and avoiding the use of mulches. It also helps to clean up dead foliage as soon as you notice it, burning the debris (see the sidebar on the facing page).

Once a rampant fungal infection gets established, it is difficult to check without resort to fungicides, so, however reluctantly, I have recommended them below. The most effective are the systemic fungicides, which are absorbed by the fungus and penetrate to all parts of it, killing it completely. Consult your local agricultural agent to learn which fungicides are currently deemed safe and are approved for use on irises in your state or province.

Crown rot
Crown rot attacks the rhizome just where the fan joins it, causing the leaves to rot away at their bases and fall over. The leaves show yellow tips and a matting of fine fungal threads where the damage has been done. The growing point of the rhizome will soon be destroyed.

Crown rot is treated much like soft rot—you scrape away all the infected tissue and allow the scraped surface to dry thoroughly. Drenching

SANITATION IS PREVENTION

The bottom line on diseases and pests of irises, as you have probably gathered by now, is simply good garden sanitation. Conduct a major cleanup of all old iris foliage and organic debris twice a year, in late fall and again in early spring. Burn it. During the spring and summer, pull off and destroy any outer leaves that wither.

Regularly replant your irises to avoid crowding, since pests thrive when they can easily move from one plant host to another, and diseases rapidly spread under conditions of poor air circulation. Site Bearded Iris plantings where they receive the longest possible period of direct sun and where drainage is excellent. Finally, a healthy, organic-rich soil produces healthy plants. Research has shown time and again that healthy plants have deep green foliage, which is less attractive to pests and is better able to resist the attacks of diseases. As much as possible, avoid using commercially prepared fertilizers, which may produce lush, susceptible growth. Try to avoid turning to insecticides and fungicides as a first resort for pest control; throughout the book I've suggested a number of other ways of dealing with these problems.

the infected plants and the surrounding soil with a systemic fungicide should complete the cure and prevent immediate recurrence. However, the small, hard sclerotia may remain viable in the soil for years and so sooner or later, when conditions are favorable, crown rot will come back. It is most destructive in warm, wet weather and in soils that are heavy and poor in organic matter.

Botrytis rot

Unlike crown rot, botrytis rot prefers cool conditions and does its dirty work in the spring. Affected plants look moldy, and unlike soft rot and crown rot, the rhizomes become dry and brown inside (instead of a healthy white). This problem usually takes care of itself, and as the weather warms and dries, botrytis disappears. One good dose of systemic fungicide, as per the instructions on the label, will cure infected plants.

If either of these fungal rots becomes a serious, recurring problem, the only solution is to dig up all the plants, treat them with a systemic fungicide, and fumigate the soil of the beds. This is something nobody wants to do. Deal with the problem while it's still possible!

LEAF SPOTS

Leaf spotting may be caused by a bacterium or a fungus. Both produce rather similar symptoms, but with practice they can be told apart. I suspect that the prevalence of leaf spotting was behind the old custom of cutting down the foliage of bearded irises after the blooming season. This practice may actually have been helpful, at least with bacterial leaf spot.

Bacterial leaf spot

Bacterial leaf spot begins at the margins or tips of the leaves and produces soft, watery areas that spread rapidly and run together, working downward through the leaf. Eventually the whole leaf may die. This form of leaf spot is relatively uncommon and occurs during long spells of wet weather. It is found mostly in northeastern North America.

The only cure is to cut off any infected leaves well below the spotted region, using tools that are dipped in a bleach solution between cuts to sterilize them. Good garden sanitation also helps; pull off any dead leaves, and don't allow irises to become so crowded that air can't easily circulate amongst them. The spread of the disease slows or stops when the weather dries off.

Fungal leaf spot
As many as eight different leaf-spot fungi attack different sorts of irises, but the symptoms are all the same. Small spots appear anywhere on a leaf (but more usually toward the tips) and grow to about ¼ in. in diameter, with a yellowish center and a distinct brown border (photo, below). The spots do not get soft and run together as in bacterial leaf spot, but they can become so abundant that the whole leaf is destroyed. Heavily infected plants are seriously weakened and will fail to thrive. Like bacterial

Fungal leaf spot is a major disease of iris foliage. Note the brown rims that ring the lesions.

leaf spot, fungal leaf spot occurs most often during wet weather. You might notice it in the eastern part of North America and in Europe in early spring.

In areas with dry summers, fungal leaf spot comes on with the autumn rains. Fortunately, systemic fungicides work quickly to limit the spread of the disease. For the sake of appearances, badly spotted leaves can be removed. Even more so than with other diseases, fungal leaf spot can be prevented by avoiding crowding (the disease spreads from plant to plant) and by cleaning up dead foliage thoroughly in the fall and burning it. Some authorities say that if you can keep this disease out for two years, it will not recur unless brought in on new plants.

IRIS MOSAIC VIRUS

Iris mosaic virus is a foliage disease that is not much of a problem for most bearded irises. Probably nearly all irises are infected with the virus and show no symptoms. Susceptible varieties and species will have foliage showing lighter areas, and flowers of these forms will be streaked with darker pigment, usually purple. The darker streaking is called "color breaking," and a similar, though more benign, virus is responsible for the streaked tulips called 'Rembrandt' tulips. In severe cases, flowers may be twisted and distorted. There's nothing you can do about it except to avoid varieties that show symptoms.

SCORCH

Scorch is an iris disease of unknown cause, and luckily it's of rather rare occurrence. Scorch has unique symptoms. Leaves at the center of the fan begin to die at the tips, but can't be pulled free of the rhizome. When the affected plant is dug up, the roots (not the rhizome!) are dead and hollow. Some cases of scorch can be treated by digging up the rhizome and letting it cure in the sun for a week or so. Whatever the scorch organism is, heat seems to destroy it. Scorch is not very contagious, and if it spreads at all, the agents are likely to be aphids (see below). Control of these insects can limit the disease.

Scorch is found mostly along the southern rim of the region in which bearded irises can be grown, stretching across the country from northern Georgia and Alabama to southern California.

Pests

There are remarkably few insect pests that attack only irises, but irises can be attacked by a variety of bugs that have broad appetites. Most gardeners are familiar with these creatures and know how to sort them out; I'll deal with the peskiest generalists first, then turn to our one major specialist, the dreaded iris borer.

APHIDS

Aphids (also called greenflies) are small green or gray insects that cluster on iris leaves and suck out sap; they also can spread disease by moving from infected plants to uninfected ones.

One easy control is mechanical. Because iris leaf fans are so two-dimensional, aphids can be wiped off simply by running the leaves between your fingers. If any clusters of aphids are destroyed this way as soon as they appear, the problem can be limited.

When lots of plants and lots of aphids are involved, the next easiest method of control is spraying with insecticidal soap (or just a weak solution of liquid dish detergent). If things get really bad, you can try a contact insecticide containing pyrethrin, which is quite safe and breaks down quickly. Fortunately we have many allies in the fight against aphids. Natural predators include ladybird beetles, green lacewings, and daddy-long-legs.

WHITEFLIES

Whiteflies are a somewhat more serious problem than aphids, but whiteflies are not usually found on irises grown outdoors except in some areas of California. As the name indicates, whiteflies are small, white insects that fly up in confused clouds when disturbed. Like aphids, they and their young suck juices from leaves. They also exude a sugary substance that supports mold, so are often accompanied by a black, smutty dust over the plants.

Whiteflies reproduce so rapidly that they are hard to control, and some kinds are resistant to insecticides. For mild infestations, try an insecticidal soap first, and if that doesn't work, switch to a pyrethrin-based insecticide. Many of the harsher, more dangerous insecticides are ineffective against whiteflies. These speedily breeding creatures have evolved multiple resistances.

NEMATODES

Nematodes are microscopic worms that are found in vast numbers in any soil. Most nematodes are harmless to plants, but others cause damage by infesting roots. In iris plants, nematodes can cause scorch-like stunting. The infestation causes distinct, tumor-like nodules to form on the roots, weakening them and limiting their ability to absorb water. Above ground, the plants look sickly, with flabby, yellowish foliage; eventually they may die.

Nematodes are more likely to be a problem in sandy soils and in warm parts of the country. They are definitely a major pest of irises in southern California. Nematicides (chemicals that kill nematodes) are available but should be used with the guidance of your local cooperative extension agent. For severe infestations, the treatment is not simple: The whole planting has to be dug up, the roots all removed and destroyed, and the rhizomes fumigated and then replanted in fumigated or solarized soil (see p. 40 for a description of the solarization process). This, too, is an operation in which you need the help and advice of your extension agent.

There is some good evidence that a nematode attack is far less common and less of a problem in soil that contains a good deal of organic matter. This is probably because the predators of nematodes, including certain fungi, can thrive in such conditions. A healthy, organic-rich soil can indeed solve many gardening problems!

IRIS BORERS

Last but not least in the pest parade is the only major specialist pest of irises. The Iris borer, *Macronoctua onusta,* is native to North America, and it probably fed on native species such as *Iris versicolor* before the arrival of Europeans, who brought bearded irises with them to this country. There is some evidence that the iris borer may feed on the roots and rhizomes of other plants as well.

Originally thought to be limited to the eastern part of the United States and adjacent Canada, iris borers have been reported from as far south as South Carolina and as far west as Iowa, Wisconsin, and Missouri; there have even been a few isolated reports from Texas, Nebraska, and the Pacific Coast. Certainly this insect is no longer limited to regions north of Washington, D. C., as once thought, since it has been a major problem in my own garden in central Virginia.

Life cycle
Iris borers are caterpillars, the larvae of a medium-sized, nondescript brownish moth. In autumn, the moths lay eggs on old iris leaves and other organic debris near iris plants. The eggs survive the winter, and when they hatch with the onset of warm weather, the tiny caterpillars search out fresh iris leaves, which are usually less than 1 ft. tall at this time.

Early on the damage is not noticeable. But as the caterpillars grow, they start attacking the edges of the younger, softer leaves near the center of the fan, notching them. These unattractive creatures are also cannibals, so as they encounter their brothers, sisters, cousins, and even perfect strangers, they devour them as well. The result is that only one half-grown larva will survive on each leaf fan and start to work its way between the sheathing leaves down toward the rhizome (photo, below left).

At this point the central leaves may be so badly damaged as to die. But unlike those affected by scorch (see p. 53), leaves killed this way easily pull away from the fan. Finally the caterpillar finds its way to the rhizome and hollows it out (photo, below right), often completely destroying it or opening the way for rot. Full-grown borers are up to 2 in. long, pinkish in appearance, and with dark brown heads.

It's now late summer. The caterpillars leave the rhizomes and enter the soil near the iris plants, where they become pupae (photo at left, p. 56).

(A pupa is a mummy-like dormant stage that allows the caterpillar to transform into a moth.) In autumn, they emerge as moths (photo at right, p. 56), mate, and lay the eggs that will cause next year's infestation.

Preventing infestations the least-toxic way
Study the borer's life cycle carefully, for it contains all the clues you need to control this voracious pest. The first vulnerable point in the cycle is the egg stage. By carefully cleaning up and burning all dead, dried iris foliage and other garden debris in the late fall (and again in the early spring), you can seriously limit the numbers of borers that will hatch.

The iris borer *(Macronoctua onusta)* is a major threat to iris plantings in much of North America. At right, a fan of iris leaves has been opened to show a young borer caterpillar at work. At far right, a mature caterpillar has completely destroyed this Louisiana Iris rhizome and is ready to move out into the soil.

Pupae of the iris borer moth (far left) are about 1 in. long and shiny brown. They are found in the soil in late summer and early fall. In the fall, the pupae develop into moths (left), which lay eggs on iris foliage and other garden debris.

A second line of defense is to monitor the center leaves of young foliage fans, watching for the notches chewed by the half-grown caterpillars. If you see notches but can't see the borer, pinch the fan between your thumb and forefinger just below the notches and continue to pinch to the base of the fan. Often you'll feel a satisfying pop when the caterpillar inside the fan is crushed.

If the caterpillar makes it to the rhizome, usually destroying its growing point along the way, you can use a third method: Skewer the invader by inserting a wire into the hole left behind. Alternatively, you can dig up the rhizome and cut it open, then deal with the caterpillar. After drying for two or three days in the sun, these cut rhizomes can be replanted in a special nursery bed, where they will often

send out new side sprouts. Watch them carefully for signs of bacterial rhizome rot (see pp. 49-50).

The last line of defense is to watch for the pupae in the soil when you replant your irises. They're about 1 in. long, dark brown, and somewhat spindle-shaped, with limited powers of movement. Destroy them!

Treating with beneficial nematodes

As many gardeners have learned over the past decade, any group of garden pests can contain species that are beneficial. So it is with nematodes. While many of these tiny, soil-dwelling roundworms are harmful to plants, including irises (see p. 54), others prey on insects, infecting and rapidly destroying them. Astute biological-control companies have been raising these insect-killing nematodes and selling them to home gardeners; they can be sprayed on plants or used as a soil drench. However, using them can be complicated since they are living animals, not chemicals, and application rates have to be carefully calculated. If successful, the nematodes will invade the bodies of certain insects, multiply rapidly, and kill them. Large numbers of additional nematodes are then released to infest other insects.

In 1997, experiments were carried out at the University of Maryland in the use of two particular species of nematode, *Steinernema carpocapsae*, marketed under the trade name Vector, and *Heterorhabditis bacteriospora*, sold under the trade name Lawn Patrol. Both species had previously been successful in fighting Japanese beetle grubs and other lawn destroyers. The researchers found that both nematodes gave good control of iris borers, with Vector killing them all, when applied at a rate of 1,000 nematodes per square inch in a 1-ft.-sq. area around the plants. Vector worked better than the insecticide dimethoate, and Lawn Patrol was just as good. These first results are very encouraging, and determined organic gardeners may want to give nematodes a try. I want to emphasize that these predatory nematodes are not the same ones that infest plants and are perfectly safe for animals and humans.

Treating with systemic insecticide
Sometimes a borer infestation becomes too great to be dealt with by least-toxic means. In such a situation, you can spray all iris plants in the garden with a systemic insecticide. (A systemic insecticide is one that is absorbed by the plant and which then kills the insects that feed on it.) There are many such commercial products on the market, but check the label and get one that contains dimethoate, which is particularly effective.

The spray should be applied according to the directions on the label when the leaves of the irises are from 4 in. to 6 in. tall, then repeated about ten days later. Even if an infestation is severe, this treatment, applied for two years running, should eliminate the borer from your garden. Borers quite often reappear, though, from neighboring gardens or in plants purchased from unreliable sources, so stay alert for borer damage and take appropriate measures. Luckily for us, the adult moths are poor fliers and not strongly attracted to lights so they don't tend to travel far.

SIBERIAN IRISES

Aside from the Tall Bearded Irises, Siberians are probably the most familiar of irises to gardeners. At least two species, *Iris siberica* and *I. sanguinea,* have long been staples in herbaceous borders. Both were thriving in the semi-abandoned garden of a house my family moved into in 1945, and according to Siberian Iris authority Currier McEwen, *I. siberica* was in cultivation by 1600.

Siberian Irises contrast with Tall Bearded Irises in many ways. Instead of the fat, yam-like rhizomes of the latter, Siberian rhizomes are generally finger sized, densely crowded, and covered with coarse, black fibers, while a mass of thick, abundantly branching white roots springs from the underside. The plants themselves are more graceful, with narrow, grass-like foliage that arches attractively, and the flowers, while smaller, are produced in such abundance that the impact of an established planting is at least as great.

A mass planting of Siberian Irises is a river of color.

However, Siberian Irises lack the vast color range of the Bearded Irises, and are to be found mostly in shades of purple, pinkish lavender, violet, and blue, as well as pristine whites. "Yellow" varieties exist, but are liable to fade to cream or white. "Red" Siberian hybrids are actually more of a wine-purple.

In the early 1960s, McEwen and others succeeded in doubling the number of chromosomes in Siberian Iris and began to introduce tetraploid varieties, with larger, broader flowers of heavier substance. Siberian fanciers, however, remain catholic in their tastes and tetraploids have by no means replaced diploids as they did so quickly among the Bearded Irises. In fact, the 1996 winner of the Morgan-Wood Medal, the top prize for Siberian Irises, was 'Shaker's Prayer', a diploid variety with small flowers of narrow form (photo at right, p. 61).

Siberian Irises fall into two natural categories, which botanists call subseries. Subseries Siberica consists of plants with a chromosome count of 28; all varieties in this group are based on two species, *I. siberica* and *I. sanguinea.* An attractive third species, *I. typhifolia,* was recently introduced to gardeners (see the sidebar below), but has not yet made much of an impact. Members of this group are highly adaptable garden plants; most Siberian Iris in commerce are of this type.

The second subseries, Chrysographes, contains perhaps eight species, all with 40 chromosomes. All native to China, they're usually referred to as Sino-Siberians. More demanding in their requirements, these irises are harder for gardeners to find but are well worth the effort in climates where they can be grown. For more about these plants, see pp. 71-73.

IRIS TYPHIFOLIA

Iris typhifolia, an early-blooming Siberian Iris species recently introduced to gardens from China.

An exciting new species, *Iris typhifolia* is a somewhat smaller, more graceful plant than either *I. siberica* or *I. sanguinea.* The leaves are narrower and in the clump almost resemble a robust grass rather than an iris. Atop wiry one- or two-branched stems, the elegant, narrow-petaled flowers are in various shades of blue-purple, some being almost true blue, and others a deep, velvety violet (photo, left). But the most surprising characteristic of this Siberian is its early season of bloom. The first flowers in my small planting of *I. typhifolia* appear just as the Miniature Dwarf Bearded Irises are fading, and other plants continue to bloom nearly to the beginning of the Standard Tall Bearded season.

Iris typhifolia is a member of the Subseries Siberica, and as such, probably has 28 chromosomes. A native of China and Mongolia, it was first collected in the late 1920s, but did not come into western gardens until 1988, when seed from China became available. I grew a number of plants of it from seeds just a few years later. I suspect that it will soon be available as plants from iris specialists.

The introduction of a new species into gardens is always a cause for rejoicing, particularly when the new plant is as attractive and adaptable as *I. typhifolia* seems to be. Besides, a new species presents a new collation of genetic material that may be of use to hybridizers. In the case of *I. typhifolia,* which readily crosses with the two related species and with garden hybrids, the most important potential is that it may be used to transfer its early blooming habits to large-flowered garden hybrids. If this can be done, *typhifolia* hybrids and the repeat-blooming Siberians will give Siberian Irises a blooming season equivalent to all of the types of Bearded Irises combined!

The Garden Hybrids

The typical modern Siberian Iris hybrid is about 30 in. tall, with the flowers held several inches above the highest foliage. (Dwarf selections, 6 in. to 10 in. tall, are also available but seem not to have caught on.) The flower stalks carry one or two branches, and each branch has one or two flower buds. The form of the flowers is quite variable, but there is a definite trend toward wider, rounder petals with some degree of ruffling, and with open, spreading standards and flaring falls. In contrast, older varieties have narrower petals, the standards fully erect and the falls held vertically. The style arms are large for the size of the flower, and sometimes show a contrasting color. Frequently, they are ornamented with feathering along the midrib. The falls may be marked at their base with a broad area of white, yellow, or green, called a signal patch.

COLOR AND PATTERN

Color and pattern, while in a somewhat restricted range, take many interesting forms, as the photos in this chapter show. Purple Siberians range from near blacks to light lavender shades that border on pink; many varieties have a distinct reddish cast, though no real reds have yet appeared. Blues are available in abundance, from the palest sky blue to rich navy, and of course there are many white varieties, some with a definite yellow or green influence on the falls, but others of absolute purity.

Selfs are the most common pattern. Bicolors, with falls darker than the standards, and amoenas, with white standards and pigmented falls, also occur, but are rare. The plicata pattern (an edging of darker color) has not appeared among Siberians, though varieties have been produced with a hairline edging on the petals, gold or silver against a blue or purple

'Jewelled Crown' (right), 1993 Morgan-Wood Medal winner, exemplifies the modern Siberian Iris with broad, ruffled form.

Species-like form and great profusion of bloom helped 'Shaker's Prayer' (far right) win the 1996 Morgan-Wood Medal.

The delicately blended shades of 'Steve Varner' invite close inspection. This variety took the Morgan-Wood Medal in 1987.

The rich plum of 'Devil's Dream' has great landscape value.

'Mabel Coday' won the Morgan-Wood Medal in 1991.

background. Others show interesting mottled and flushed patterns or are marked by strong, dark veining against a lighter background.

Unfortunately, efforts to bring the more varied color range and patterns of the subseries Chrysographes into the modern hybrids have not been very successful so far. The great difference in chromosome number is a significant barrier.

BLOOMING SEASON

Typically, Siberian Irises bloom at about the same time as the Tall Bearded hybrids and continue a little later. *Iris typhifolia,* however, blooms very early and may accompany the Standard Dwarf Bearded Irises.

One of the most exciting developments to appear in Siberian Irises has been that of repeat-blooming varieties. Repeat blooming differs from reblooming in the bearded irises in that repeat-blooming Siberians bloom again after just a short rest, rather than waiting until fall. The tendency is highly variable. Some repeaters do so only occasionally, others nearly always, and still others bloom more heavily during the second period than the first. A few varieties even bloom more or less continuously without resting, going on for a very long season. Currier McEwen has experimented with this trait, and it is definitely genetic, so it can be passed on and selected for. I expect that in a decade or two, it will become standard for Siberian Irises to show repeat bloom or to be continous bloomers.

SOURCES FOR PLANTS

There are fewer specialist nurseries for Siberians than for Bearded Irises (see pp. 162-165), but at least some older varieties of Siberians can be found in the catalogs of many general nurseries, and local garden centers often carry Siberians in pots. Choosing varieties might be more difficult because specialist catalogs usually do not contain color photographs, only verbal descriptions of the varieties they offer. Therefore, a visit to an established planting or nursery is very helpful in making a selection.

General Cultural Requirements

As widely adapted as they are, Siberians will not grow everywhere. Gardeners in the lowland southern states will have problems keeping them happy, but they will thrive in the cooler climes of the southern mountains. Similarly, arid conditions are hard on Siberians, and while they will grow beautifully in many parts of the southwestern United States, much extra attention is required. In New England, the Middle Atlantic States, the upper Midwest and the Pacific Northwest, they will be trouble-free, outstanding performers. In southern Canada, particularly in the Maritime Provinces, beautiful, free-flowering clumps will form quickly, and there have been reports of success even in Alaska.

This information makes sense when we consider where the two progenitor species of these varieties live. Despite its name, *Iris siberica* is a native of central Europe, but its range extends well into Russia, even as far as the shores of Lake Baikal in Central Asia. *Iris sanguinea* (photo, below) is found in Siberia, Korea, Japan, and northeastern China. Throughout their ranges, both species are subject to extreme cold and heavy snow cover, so we can conclude that cold hardiness is no problem. Both species are found most commonly as meadow plants, competing successfully with herbs and grasses, but enjoying full exposure to the sun and abundant moisture at their roots.

Iris sanguinea, with its purple-based foliage, is found in many older gardens.

SEASONS FOR PLANTING

Like nearly all beardless irises, Siberians never become completely dormant during their growing season, though growth slows down in fall as winter approaches. The roots of the plants must never be allowed to dry out, so instead of being shipped dry in well-ventilated containers, Siberians usually arrive with their roots packed in damp peat and enclosed in a plastic bag, or as containerized plants.

Their more or less continous growth program also means that depending on where you live, there are two seasons when Siberian Irises can be planted. For gardeners in the North, spring planting is favored. Spring-planted Siberians will have the mild, moist summer period to establish themselves; if planted in the fall, the freezing and thawing of winter may prove fatal to the unestablished plants. In the South, though, spring planting is less secure since hot weather arrives quickly and summers may be dry. It is far better to plant in the fall, when the long, usually wet transition to winter will permit abundant root growth.

The bottom line? Specify spring shipment in the North, fall shipment in the South. Siberian specialist nurseries will be happy to make the choice for you. Even if these instructions are followed, Siberians often will not bloom the year after planting, and may make a considerable clump before the first flowers appear. Containerized plants—perhaps available locally, but not usually supplied by mail-order nurseries—are more adaptable, but still thrive best when set out at the appropriate time.

DISPLAY OR BORDER?

While collectors may want to mass their Siberians in dedicated beds, many gardeners prefer to use them as border plants, for which they are ideal (top photo, facing page). Because they derive from natives of meadows, their competitive abilities are greater than those of most other irises, and indeed it may be neccessary to protect other kinds of plants in a border from encroachment by the Siberian Irises. After the flowers have passed, their graceful, healthy foliage continues to contribute to the overall picture. Daylilies, columbines, lilies, delphiniums and monkshood, as well as many other border stalwarts, are good companions for Siberian Irises.

SUN AND MOISTURE

Exposure is important. More sun means more bloom and healthier plants, but Siberian Irises are surprisingly tolerant of shade. I've seen old varieties growing—and still blooming—almost completely shaded in overgrown shrubberies, but this is not a recommendation. While full sun is important in northern regions, some midday shade may improve performance in the South. In the desert Southwest, just a half a day of sun will produce abundant blooms.

Good drainage is vital, especially in winter, but there must be a steady supply of soil moisture. Unlike some other kinds of beardless irises, Siberians will not survive standing in water while they are dormant, and such conditions are not to be recommended even when the plants are in vigorous growth. Even so, a position just up from the shore of a pond or the

Siberian Irises are quite adaptable. They make excellent border subjects with companion plants that bloom at the same time (above). They can also thrive by the waterside (right).

banks of a stream, where the iris's roots can always find water but the rhizomes are dry, is touted as ideal by the experts (bottom photo, p. 65). Just keep that image of a moist mountain meadow in mind.

PREPARING THE SOIL

Soil preparation, whether of a dedicated bed or a spot in the border, should be deep and thorough, since Siberian Irises do not require transplanting for up to five years. Dig and prepare the soil about a month before planting the irises, so that the mellowing process may occur, with its consequent increase in beneficial soil microbes. Soils that are slightly acidic and rich in organic matter serve these irises best. Because an acid pH is preferred, rotted ground bark, sawdust, oak or pine leaf mold, and other acidic soil amendments can be used.

Three- to five-rhizome divisions are usually supplied by mail-order nurseries.

Some experts recommend digging in a good deal of peat moss in preparing for Siberian Irises, and certainly this would improve the soil texture and do no harm. Peat moss, however, is not a very good substrate for soil microorganisms because it breaks down so slowly as to contribute few nutrients. Once again, the best choice is thoroughly prepared compost. Siberian Irises are not gross feeders, and if the soil is prepared properly with a good supply of organic matter, they should never require fertilizer from a bag.

PLANTING INSTRUCTIONS

When plants arrive in the mail, they will be packed in damp peat moss in plastic bags. Each plant is (or should be) supplied as a division with three to five growing and healthy rhizomes (photo, below left); single divisions are harder to establish. Never, never let the roots of the plants dry out. In fact, they will benefit from being unpacked and submerged in a bucket of water overnight before planting.

The planting hole should be deep and wide enough to allow the roots of the division to be well spread out and to descend into the soil at an acute angle, so the newly set division will be well-anchored. Siberian rhizomes should be completely buried, with the crown of the plant about 1 in. deep. Fill in the hole and carefully firm the soil, then water thoroughly to settle the soil even more and to ensure that your new plants get plenty of moisture. If nature does not oblige, be sure the irises get at least 1 in. of water per week until they are established.

The importance of mulch

Unlike their bearded cousins, Siberians appreciate a mulch year-round. If you are planting in the spring, the mulch will conserve moisture and contribute mightily toward the establishment of your new irises. If fall planting is in order, the mulch will protect against that deadly freeze/thaw cycle, and by delaying the freezing of the soil, it will give the plants that much longer to establish a good root system. The mulch can be applied right after planting.

The ideal mulch is light in texture. Good choices are pine straw, coarse ground bark, and partially decayed leaf mold. Avoid using grass clippings, freshly fallen autumn leaves, or peat moss, the first two because they pack down and potentially smother the soil, the last because it can dry out and form a nearly impervious crust that prevents the penetration of water.

Spring and summer growth

In spring, the fresh green shoots of Siberian Irises appear early and grow quickly. The new foliage will be stiff and erect. Flowers stalks will begin to appear about at the peak season for Tall Bearded Iris bloom (which ranges from March and April in the South and California to late June and early July in New England). The Siberian peak comes a short time later, carrying the iris season on for a few weeks more. Repeat-blooming varieties will extend the enjoyment even longer.

Siberian Irises do not usually require fertilization, but older, crowded clumps may benefit from an acid-type fertilizer just before the bloomstalks appear. Look for the kinds recommended for azaleas, rhododendrons,

and hollies. Sprinkle very lightly around the edges of the clump; do not allow the dry fertilizer to come into contact with fresh green growth. Through the summer, watering from time to time is also beneficial, because Siberians prefer their roots to be constantly moist. Mulches may also need to be renewed.

Siberian Irises readily form seed pods; one will appear in the place of nearly every flower. Unless seed is wanted, these should be removed to channel strength into the formation of new rhizomes. If the seed pods are allowed to mature, prepare for a spate of seedlings to spring up everywhere in the vicinity of the parent clump. Since these seedlings are often at the same time more vigorous and less attractive than their parents, they tend to overpower their elders, and treasured varieties may be replaced by something much less desirable (this is the source of the untrue legend that Siberian Irises "revert" after years in the garden).

The stalks of Siberians cannot be easily broken or pulled from the rhizomes, but instead should be cut off close to the ground. This is a separate operation from removing the seed pods and should be performed later.

Preparing for winter

In autumn, the foliage of Siberians tends to be fairly persistant, and I have found that it is not a good idea to cut it down while it is still green. This practice seems to inhibit blooming the following spring; it may be that a natural maturation process is needed in order to set buds. When the foliage finally does turn brown, cut it off close to ground level and burn it.

Siberian Iris foliage does not pull away from the rhizome easily, and in attempting to do so you risking yanking up the plant itself. After the first year, winter protection is unnecessary; Siberian hybrids are rock hardy in even the coldest climates.

Dividing and Replanting

Given good conditions, all Siberian Irises will multiply rapidly and form large, dense clumps (photo, below left). Regularly supplementing mulches, I have had some clumps in the same position for a decade without any diminution of bloom. Frequently, however, the center of the clump will die out in the normal course of events, and the crowding of the new rhizomes will result in reduced performance. At this point it is necesary to divide and replant. In the North, this is best done soon after the bloom season, when new roots are forming and the plants are growing vigorously. In the South, fall is the best time for this work, since plants newly divided and set out in early summer may have trouble establishing themselves in hot, dry weather.

DIGGING UP AN OLD CLUMP

Begin by cutting down the foliage to between one-third and one-half of its length (photo, below right). This will balance the root loss that is about to occur and also make the rhizomes easier to see and handle.

Large, crowded clumps of Siberian Irises are a formidable challenge to uproot, and a stout, short-handled spading fork is required. Sinking in the fork about 6 in. outside the clump, work around and around, gradually loosening the huge mass of roots. Eventually, the clump will be uprooted with a minimal loss of live, white

This crowded clump of the Siberian Iris variety 'Silver Edge' is ready to be divided.

To make digging easier, the foliage is first trimmed to 8 in. or 10 in.

1.

2.

3.

Slicing the Pie

1. **Using a sharp spade, cut out a triangular section from the edge of the clump.**

2. **Lift the cut section with a spading fork.**

3. **Remove the cut section from the main clump.**

4. **Fill in the wedge with compost where the section was removed.**

4.

feeder roots. Once the roots have been exposed to air, you need to work quickly lest they dry out and die. Keep a hose handy to wet them down as the process continues.

Much as is recommended in dividing daylilies, the clump can be broken up into manageable divisions by using two spading forks placed back to back and worked against each other until the separation occurs. These large pieces can then be pulled apart further by hand. Ideally, one should reset pieces with no more than a dozen active rhizomes, and no fewer than three.

Soil preparation and planting technique follows the same guidelines as for newly acquired plants (see p. 66). Inevitably, there will be a lot of plant material left over, and if this is not to be discarded, it should be kept in a bucket or tub of water until it can be given away or sold.

ANOTHER WAY TO DIVIDE SIBERIAN IRIS

Established Siberian Iris clumps can be so beautiful that we are often reluctant to break them up completely to replant, as I've described above. An alternative method that has worked well for me is to use a sharp spade to cut a pie-shaped section from the margin of the clump. This cluster of active new rhizomes can then be loosened with a spading fork and removed and the gap can be filled with compost (photos, p. 69). If this is done on four or five sides of an established clump, the old clump is reinvigorated by the fresh compost at its roots, and the new divisions can be planted elsewhere in the garden.

Cut sections should be kept in a basin of water until they can be replanted elsewhere in the garden.

Keep a bucket or basin of water handy to receive the new divisions, so that they do not dry out while waiting to be replanted (photo, below). You can leave them in the bucket for as long as a week, and they will send out fresh white roots. The foliage needs to be cut only on the divisions that have been removed, so the rhizomes left behind are not significantly set back and will surely bloom the next year.

Diseases and Pests

Of all the irises, Siberians are the least troubled by diseases and pests, and rarely require any attention at all on that score.

FUNGAL ROTS

Some of the same fungal rhizome rots that attack Bearded Irises (see pp. 50-51) also can, from time to time, attack Siberian Irises, but are much less frequent and often self-limiting. Botrytis rot shows up in the spring; the outermost leaves of a fan turn brown at the tips and fall over. Near the base of the fallen leaves, fungal webbing can be seen, and the leaves are easily pulled away. Systemic fungicides are effective in severe cases (which are very rare), but usually as the weather dries out, the disease disappears on its own. Crown rot has similar symptoms, but appears in warm weather. There have been very few reports of this disease in Siberians; systemic fungicides clean it up quickly. Bacterial soft rot has never been a problem in Siberians.

YELLOWING FOLIAGE

The foliage of Siberian Irises is unusually healthy and free from disfiguring disease. Neither fungal nor bacterial leaf spot infects these irises. In soils that are too alkaline, there may sometimes be too little available iron for Siberian Irises, and the leaves will develop a mottled yellow appearance. Chelated iron, available at garden supply centers, can be used as a supplement, and a mulch of acidic material, such as pine needles, may be all that's needed to adjust the soil pH.

SCORCH

The mysterious disease scorch (treated more fully on p. 53) sometimes hits Siberians. Center leaves of the fan brown at the tips, but remain firmly attached to the rhizome. Plants attacked by scorch rarely recover, but the disease does not spread from plant to plant, except perhaps as it might be carried by sucking insects such as aphids. Since there seems to be no cure, dig out and destroy scorched plants if they appear.

IRIS BORERS

Among insects, only the iris borer is likely to attack the foliage or rhizomes of Siberian Irises, but these plants not a very satisfactory meal for the insect because of their small rhizomes. As discussed on pp. 54-57, the borer is the caterpillar of a rather weak, dull moth, which lays its eggs in the fall on iris foliage. After entering a leaf fan and destroying one Siberian rhizome, the caterpillar may move to attack adjacent rhizomes and thus do a good deal of damage.

Prevention is the best cure; clean up and burn withered foliage. If numbers of leaf fans show notched edges or yellowed center leaves that easily pull out of the fan, spray with a dimethoate-containing systemic insecticide. A single treatment is usually effective.

IRIS BUD FLIES

The maggot of a small fly, the iris bud fly, may sometimes eat parts of Siberian Iris flowers. If flowers are damaged and small, white maggots are seen, cut off the damaged flowers with a short length of stem and destroy them.

The Sino-Siberians

Earlier in the chapter, I mentioned that there are two groups of Siberian Irises. Because the garden favorites all belong to the Subseries Siberica, much of what I've written so far applies to them. The Subseries Chrysographes, however, is worth considering, especially for mild climates. Because plants in this group hail from China, they're also called Sino-Siberians.

Some of the species in the Chrysographes group, such as *Iris forrestii* (top photo, p. 72) and *I. wilsonii*, carry genes for yellow pigment, a color not usually found among the more popular garden Siberians.

Iris chrysographes itself is one of the most striking of all irises (photo, bottom left), and the only one of the subseries commonly grown in gardens. Its petals range from rich reddish violet to close to black in some selections. Most of these are marked at the base of the falls with brilliant gold dashes, hence the species name, which means "golden writing."

Another very worthy species is *I. delavayi,* in shades of violet-blue with a white signal patch, often with a pattern of dark blue lines over the falls (photo, bottom right). Blooming very late in the season, often with or just before the Japanese Irises, *I. delavayi* can send up bloomstalks over 5 ft. tall!

The Chinese *Iris forrestii* is one of only two yellow-flowering species among Siberian Irises.

Iris chrysographes (far left) varies from deep wine to nearly black, but almost always has distinctive golden "writing" on the falls. It is a Siberian Iris species with 40 chromosomes.

Iris delavayi (left), another Sino-Siberian, grows quite tall (to 4 ft.) and blooms the latest of all Siberian Irises.

With the exception of *I. delavayi*, the members of the Chrysographes subseries produce smaller rhizomes and thinner, more drooping foliage than those of the Siberica subsection. Originating as they do in the high mountains of southern China, these species require cool, moist summers and mild winters. They do splendidly in the Pacific Northwest and in the milder regions of Britain.

Few named hybrids are available, but since all the members of the series cross easily with the others, even plants labeled as being a particular species can turn out to be a surprise, usually a pleasant one.

'Half Magic', a Calsibe hybrid, makes a spectacular clump.

THE CALIFORNIA CONNECTION

As it happens, the chromosome numbers of the Chrysographes subseries and the Pacific Coast Native Irises are the same (see pp. 140-143 for a discussion of the latter). The two groups can be crossed with each other, and the results, called Calsibes, are extraordinarily beautiful and varied (photo, above right).

Unluckily, though, both of the parent groups are of somewhat limited adaptability. More selection for tolerance of unfavorable conditions will be needed before they can become more than collector's items away from the favored climates of the Pacific Northwest and the British Isles.

GROWING SINO-SIBERIANS

The information on pp. 63-68 needs only a little modification to apply to the Sino-Siberians. In general the same conditions will grow good clumps of both groups, but the Chrysographes types definitely need more moisture and a steady supply of it. This is especially true in climates with hot summers.

My personal experience is limited to *Iris chrysographes*, *I. delavayi* (a beautiful iris more robust than the others of the subseries), and complex hybrids raised from seed. Here in the midst of USDA hardiness Zone 7a, these irises are short-lived perennials. The problem is clearly summer heat and drought; we can only do something about the latter. Members of this subseries are not as hardy to cold as the more available Siberians, and will generally not survive winters north of Zone 5.

LOUISIANA IRISES

Early in this century, a small, dedicated group of gardeners from the bayou country of Louisiana began collecting native irises from the swamps and fields and transplanting them into their gardens. The variety of color and form of these home-grown wildflowers was almost unbelievable; botanist John Small called Louisiana "the iris center of the universe." Through the 1920s and 1930s, Small went on to name scores of different species from the region, based on the extraordinary diversity he saw, both in the wild and in local gardens. Alas for Small, later botanists found that most of his species were in fact naturally occurring hybrids, and today only five species of Louisiana Irises are recognized (see pp. 77-78). The vast numbers of variants resulted from the fact that these five species are fully interfertile and cross with one another very easily; many generations of interbreeding resulted in botanical chaos.

Though attention has focused on Louisiana as the center of development of these irises, the five species actually have wider ranges, and at least two of them wander up the Mississippi

Louisiana Iris 'Frosted Morn' in a planting with yellow *Iris pseudacorus* 'Beuron'.

River valley to Indiana and Ohio, while another can be found in Florida, Georgia, and South Carolina. Although their native haunts tend to be swampy, the species and their hybrids do very well under ordinary garden conditions.

The Plants

A typical Louisiana Iris grows from a large, elongated, knotty rhizome that is usually not exposed on the surface of the ground. The rhizomes grow rapidly, and large clumps quickly form, often "walking" a good distance from where they were originally planted. From each rhizome springs a broad fan of robust, heavy-textured, bright green foliage. Individual fans of leaves are nearly 3 ft. tall. When held to the light, the long, parallel veins can be seen to be connected by cross-links, called "water marks" (photo at left, p. 76). These supposedly indicate a fondness for moisture and even a tolerance of standing water.

Bloomstalks emerge from the fans and may top out 6 in. to 8 in. above the foliage, but some robust varieties, if well grown, can exceed a height of 5 ft. The stalks are usually generously branched, though the branches may curve back toward the main stalk or be quite short. Each branch and the terminal carry one, two, or three buds, which open in succession to give a season of bloom about the same as that of a Tall Bearded variety, and as is the case with those irises, Louisiana Iris bloomstalks may carry three or four open flowers at the same time.

The Flowers

A typical garden hybrid will have a flower about 6 in. across. The flowers themselves have the delightful array of forms often found in plants not far removed from their progenitor species, and can be narrow and spidery, or with petals so broad as to be overlapping.

Some Louisiana Irises show typical iris form, with erect standards and pendant falls (photo, below right). The falls and standards are usually rather similar in size, and most kinds have standards broadly spreading, even lying flat, as do the flaring falls. The falls may or may not have a strong triangular or spearhead-shaped signal patch of bright yellow. The style arms are short and stout. Strongly ruffled petal edges are a popular feature of newer varieties. 'Creole Can-Can', with extra petals, was found among natural hybrids in the wild, and has produced a race of true doubles, in contrast to other so-called double irises in which the standards are replaced by another set of falls (this condition also occurs in Louisiana Irises). The substance of the flowers is remarkable, and they withstand hot weather and rain with ease.

The short, dark cross-veins in this Louisiana Iris leaf (above) are a sign that the plant will do well in wet ground or standing water. Similar "water marks" are found in other wetland irises.

'Dr. Dormon' (right) shows typical Louisiana Iris form.

Louisiana Iris 'Easter Morn' (above): a delicate bicolor blending of pale violet and creamy yellow.

A mass planting of 'Ann Chowning' in the author's garden (left) highlights the approach to true red in Louisiana Irises.

Louisiana Irises have the greatest color range of any iris group, including the closest approaches to true red in the entire genus. White, purple, blue, violet, red, pink, orange, yellow, brown, and many shades and combinations of these colors are available. Bicolor, bitone, amoena, and plicata patterns have all appeared in Louisiana Irises (see pp. 25-27 for definitions of these terms). Some varieties feature strong veining of a contrasting color to the rest of the petal (photo at left, p. 78). In some combinations, such as red-violet on yellow, the overall look is a coppery effect when the flowers are seen from a distance.

The Family Album

The natural habitat of the original five species of Louisiana Irises, which botanists call the Series Hexagonae, is in the swamps, river bottoms, and bayous of the Mississippi and Ohio River Valleys and the Gulf Coast, skipping peninsular Florida to occur again from southern Georgia into South Carolina. The five generally acknowledged species are all beautiful plants and good garden subjects in their own right, and so worth a brief description.

The Series Hexagonae is named for *Iris hexagona,* found in the lowlands of the Florida panhandle, Georgia, and South Carolina.

'C'est Si Bon' shows a heavily veined pattern with a fine white edge to the fall petals.

Iris fulva is the only red iris species, and the source of red in Louisiana Iris hybrids. Here it contrasts with a much larger modern hybrid seedling.

Flowering in shades of purple and blue, and an attractive plant well adapted to the southeastern coastal plain (I grew it during a brief stay in central Florida), *I. hexagona* has nonetheless contributed little to the development of the modern hybrids. Most of that work took place in Louisiana, where *I. hexagona* is not found.

Iris brevicaulis is a rather short-stemmed species, but the bloomstalks are distinctively zigzagged, so the opening flowers do not interfere with each other. This species is known for its beautiful blue shades, and since it grows as far north as Ohio, Illinois, and Indiana, it is also quite cold hardy. In southern Louisiana, it has hybridized extensively with the following two species, giving rise to the many forms that intrigued early collectors.

Iris giganticaerulea can be found only in southern Louisiana, particularly along the coast, and may be somewhat tolerant of brackish water. Its color is highly variable, but always in shades of blue and violet, ranging through to white. It grows up to 5 ft. tall under good conditions, with huge rhizomes. The genes of this iris clearly dominate in most of the garden hybrids.

Red, orange, and yellow tones in Louisiana Irises come from *Iris fulva,* the only known red-flowering species of the genus (photo, above right). Like *I. brevicaulis,* this species ranges far to the north of the Gulf Coast, into Arkansas and Ohio, and has contributed hardiness as well as its unique color.

The fifth Louisiana Iris species, *I. nelsonii,* is limited to a small area around Abbeville, Louisiana, and according to botanists, arose as a hybrid of *fulva* and *giganticaerulea.* It has the color range of *fulva,* with the added bonus of rich purples, but the size of *giganticaerulea.*

Hybridization in the wild

Four of the five species hybridized extensively among themselves in southern Louisiana, and the hybrids also crossed with each other and with the parent species. The memoirs of collectors such as Caroline Dormon speak of vast fields of irises in a seemingly endless variety of colors and forms. From collections made by the early pioneers, plant breeders have wrought tremendous improvements in Louisiana Irises in only a few decades. And just in the nick of time, too, because development, highway building, and industrialization have forever destroyed the iris fields of southern Louisiana. A few populations hang on tenuously here and there, but to collect irises now would be an ecological crime of serious dimensions. Efforts must be made to preserve the few remaining stands.

The development of tetraploid varieties

Recently, largely through the work of Joseph Mertzweiler, tetraploid Louisiana Irises have appeared. They were artificially induced, using the drug colchicine. Because only a few plants were originally converted by this difficult process, the genetic resources available to tetraploids are limited, but new kinds are continually being introduced. The first white tetraploid appeared in 1995.

The degree of difference between the tetraploid varieties and the standard diploids is not as great as with the Tall Bearded Irises (see the sidebar on pp. 34-35), but tetraploid Louisianas are more robust than diploid Louisianas, with larger, more heavily substanced flowers and rich colors. It remains to be seen if a total shift to tetraploids will take place in the next few years, but given the high quality of available diploids, it seems unlikely.

The unnamed Louisiana Iris seedling at right is a tetraploid, with larger, more heavily substanced flowers than are found in diploids.

'It's Cool' (far right), a diploid, is a beautifully formed Louisiana Iris with slightly ruffled petal edges.

General Cultural Requirements

Louisiana Irises require moist, acidic soils, and can even grow in shallow standing water, making them ideal pool and streamside plants. The soils in which they are usually found growing are rich in organic muck, and were mostly heavy clays to begin with (an exception is *I. hexagona,* with does well in sand). Acid pH is indicated by the tea-colored waters of the southern swamps and bogs.

While hardiness can be variable, most of the garden varieties, and certainly the species *brevicaulis* and *fulva,* are cold hardy to at least USDA Zone 6. Some varieties, even though of southern origin, have successfully been grown in the awesome Zone 5 climate of South Dakota! However, according to Joseph Mertzweiler, a leading authority on these irises, they may not be well adapted to interior New England, New York, and northern Pennsylvania, and to the Pacific Northwest. While they can be grown in the arid Southwest, special soil preparation and heavy watering are required. Mertzweiler ranks California, with its mild climate, and the Gulf Coast as the premier areas for growing Louisiana Irises.

In my own garden here in central Virginia (USDA Zone 7a), Louisiana Irises are the most vigorous of all the irises I grow, and they bloom abundantly and without fail each year. I would recommend Louisianas to those southern gardeners who have had difficulties with Tall Bearded Irises due to summer heat and high humidity.

It is this surprisingly wide range of adaptability that is responsible for the extraordinary growth in popularity of Louisiana Irises in the last three decades. They have also become favorites in Australia and Japan, but in most of Europe, including Britain, Louisianas have not caught on.

SELECTING A SITE

Louisiana Irises are strong-growing, robust plants that do well either in beds of their own or in moist borders with other plants that enjoy the same conditions yet will not overwhelm the irises. They seem to find ideal companions in daylilies, and self-seeding annuals spring up easily among the rather open clumps to provide color for the late summer. If kept under control, various *Lysimachia* species are also good with Louisiana Irises.

Because Louisiana Irises are natural swamp plants, a wet situation suits them well. They will be at their most luxuriant and vigorous in a low, soggy spot, provided the soil is fertile and contains a great deal of organic matter. Natural low places and depressions often are wettest in the spring and fall, and drier through the summer and winter—thus they mimic the natural habitat of these plants.

The margin of a pond is another ideal habitat for these irises. If the rhizomes are planted above the water level, the roots can easily reach saturated soil, or, alternatively, the rhizomes themselves can be set in 2 in. to 4 in. of water. However, in northern regions where the pond or pool is likely to freeze over, planting in water is not a good idea unless the pond level can be drawn down in winter to uncover the iris clumps, which should then be mulched well.

SUN AND SHADE

Louisiana Irises, like nearly all other irises, thrive on sun, and the amount of bloom is directly related to the hours of full sun the plants get. However, there are some indications that Louisiana Irises are at least as tolerant of shade as Siberian Irises. In areas such as the southwestern United States, some protection from the fierce midday glare of the sun may be beneficial.

At the same time, Louisianas are poor competitors with the surface roots of trees, which efficiently vacuum up most of the moisture and nutrients from areas they invade. Maples are especially pernicious in this respect; pines are less so. The best place for Louisiana Irises seems to be either a dedicated bed of their own in the open, away from competing trees, or in a sunny mixed border with other plants that appreciate extra moisture.

DRAINAGE

Soil drainage is not a big problem for Louisianas, at least during their growing season, when they are perfectly happy even with a few inches of standing water over their rhizomes. However, the swamps of the Gulf Coast experience a dry season in the winter, and the water level falls dramatically, leaving irises and other plants high and dry during their dormant period. So if these plants are to be sited by the waterside, provisions should be made to drop the water level in the winter. All indications are that letting the plants freeze in ice during winter is fatal.

SOIL PREPARATION

As with any other perennial plant, soil preparation is of supreme importance in growing Louisiana Irises. The key is the incorporation of abundant organic matter, which will enhance the water-holding capacity of light soils and open the texture of clay. Organic matter is the natural food of beneficial

A bitone Louisiana Iris, 'Bayou Mystique'.

soil microbes, whose activities will provide much, if not all, of the nutrients needed by your plants.

Well-seasoned compost is undoubtedly best, but rotted leaves and pine needles, decayed wood chips, sawdust or bark, and even peat moss also work well. In the Deep South it is sometimes possible to obtain native sedge peat, an excellent soil additive for these irises. Louisiana Irises do best in heavy soils, with their generally higher fertility and moisture-retaining qualities, a virtue that adapts these irises well to the reddish, acid clays of the South.

ESTABLISHING A NEW BED

Soil for a dedicated Louisiana Iris bed should be excavated to a depth of at least 1 ft. If possible, reserve the dug-out soil and till organic matter into the bottom of the bed. Then, while replacing the excavated soil, mix in organic matter in a proportion of about one part organic matter to two parts old soil. Allow the soil to settle and mellow for a month or two. Don't be concerned if the settling process leaves the surface of the bed below the level of the surrounding ground. The sunken bed will actually benefit your Louisiana Irises by collecting water and keeping them moist during dry spells.

In much of the southwestern part of the United States, an arid climate and soils of an alkaline reaction would make it nearly impossible to grow moisture-loving plants which prefer an acid soil, without heroic measures involving watering and continual adjustment of soil pH with aluminum sulfate

and other chemicals. For enthusiasts who want to grow Louisiana Irises in regions where soils are dry and alkaline, the solution may be an **acid bed** (see the sidebar on the facing page).

TWO SEASONS OF GROWTH

Along the Gulf Coast, irises experience two seasons of growth. From early spring on, abundant moisture and warming temperatures trigger rapid sprouting of the rhizomes, and bloom follows quickly. However, the higher temperatures and the often drier weather of summer results in a slowing or cessation of growth, though there is no dieback of the leaves.

The second period of growth begins with the arrival of the fall rains and continues as long as temperatures remain mild; in the southernmost portion of their range and in parts of California, Louisiana Irises may grow through the winter. Where winter frosts and freezes are common, the foliage dies back almost to the rhizome, and the plants become completely dormant. At this point, snow cover is deemed beneficial for its insulating effect.

Of course, the flowering season varies with latitude. In the Gulf Coast region, Louisiana irises bloom as early as April, continuing on nearly into June. Here in central Virginia, their season overlaps with the Tall Bearded Irises, the late TBs flowering with early Louisianas. This provides a rough rule of thumb for estimating the blooming season in other regions. Like the Tall Bearded Irises, the season of bloom is rather short, running about three to five weeks. Rebloom and repeat bloom rarely occur in Louisiana Irises. Rebloom is limited mostly to mild regions of southern California.

THE ACID BED

The acid bed is essentially an enormous container that isolates the soil and plants within from alkali and also retains moisture. The advantage of the acid bed is that a plastic liner retains water within the bed, making for much more efficient (and therefore less costly) use of water, and the acid soil amendments are not continually being leached away. Lined beds like this are used in dry and alkaline regions, such as the Southwest. They are also useful if you want to grow Louisiana Irises near or among trees—the liner prevents the invasion of competitive tree roots.

Start by laying out the bed on the ground, either measuring with stakes and string for a rectangular planting or using a garden hose to outline a freeform shape. Remove the soil from this area to a depth of about 18 in., and discard it. Then line the excavation with heavy horticultural plastic film, which you can purchase at any garden center. It is best to use a single piece, if possible, to avoid seams, which may leak. To protect the plastic from being punctured by rocks or sticks, or while digging plants, cover it with a thick layer of folded newspapers.

Fill the lined bed with a soil mix composed of peat moss, manure, compost, sand, and perhaps even a small amount of the excavated soil. Rock phosphate, cottonseed meal, and blood meal make good nutritional supplements, but commercial granulated fertilizers, such as lawn fertilizers, should be avoided. Water thoroughly and allow the mix to settle and mellow for a few weeks before planting. Then add Louisiana Irises (or other plants that like swampy, acid conditions).

Frequent flooding of the bed provides the wet conditions Louisiana Irises prefer. A 4-in.-dia. section of plastic pipe can be inserted vertically while the bed is being filled, with its lower end about 1 in. above the plastic liner. You can look into the pipe to inspect the water level in the bed; about 1 in. of standing water should be visible in the bottom of the pipe at all times.

In many Southwestern states, the water may be strongly alkaline. If this is the case, you'll need to add horticultural sulfur to the bed to maintain the acid pH. In addition, evaporation from the surface of the bed may result in mineral salts being deposited in its upper layers. If this becomes a problem, the soil can be removed and replaced.

In such a bed, the irises should be replanted at least every three years, and new organic matter should be added to the soil mix. It is recommended that about one-third of the soil be replaced when you replant.

Sounds like quite a project, doesn't it? Fortunately, many Louisiana Iris growers in Texas, New Mexico, and Arizona find they can get along without an acid bed simply by adding a great deal of organic material, horticultural sulfur, or aluminum sulfate to their existing soil. Maintaining the soil is an ongoing process, and should be accompanied by frequent soil tests.

PLANTING THE RHIZOMES

Knowing that Louisiana Irises have two growth periods suggests planting in either spring or fall. Spring planting works best in the North, allowing the plants to become established during the mild, moist summer. In fact, Louisianas planted in the spring may even bloom the same year. Gardeners in the South should plant in late summer or fall. If the rhizomes planted are large enough, they will bloom the following spring.

To select varieties of Louisiana Irises, it may be necessary to visit a public garden, a nursery, or a private planting to view them, since most specialist nurseries do not feature color photographs in their catalogs. Specialist nurseries will ship plants in either the spring or fall. Louisiana Irises arrive from the nursery packed in plastic bags of damp peat, since the roots cannot be allowed to dry out. When your irises arrive, be sure to keep the roots moist. An overnight soak in cool water before planting will be beneficial.

As with all irises, spacing is important for Louisiana Irises; it will determine how soon you will have to divide and reset the plants. Remember that Louisiana Iris rhizomes grow rapidly and can in a single season extend themselves some distance from where they were planted. For most varieties, plant single divisions on 2-ft. centers. This spacing will give you three to four years of bloom before crowding begins to diminish it.

Louisiana Iris rhizomes must not be exposed on the surface, but should be planted from 1 in. to 3 in. deep. The reason for this is that the upper surfaces of the rhizomes are susceptible to being scalded by the sun, which can provide an avenue for the entry of rhizome rot organisms (see p. 86). Rhizomes that come in the mail may have few roots, but these should be well spread out in planting. New roots will appear quickly.

Pack the soil firmly around newly set plants and water very thoroughly. Watering is very important to the establishment of Louisiana Iris plants, especially spring-planted ones that may have to face the hotter, drier summer weather not fully established. Fall-planted rhizomes usually get enough water from rains, but at least 2 in. of water a week would not be harmful. Even fall-planted irises will quickly show new growth.

MULCHING

Mulching is absolutely vital to Louisiana Irises that are being grown in garden beds and borders. A mulch will help to conserve water and protect the rhizomes from sun-scald, and when it eventually decays it will further enrich and acidify the soil. Pine needles make an ideal mulch, as do well-chopped autumn leaves (rake them into a pile and run your lawnmower over them several times) and leaf mold. Ground bark and well-rotted sawdust will also suffice, but peat moss should be avoided as a mulch since it can dry out and form an impermeable crust that actually sheds water. As a general rule, select mulching materials that are coarse in texture and will break down in about a year.

A summer mulch should be maintained at a depth of about 3 in., but in northerly areas, where freezing weather is expected during the winter, the depth should be increased to 8 in. or 10 in. before really cold weather sets in. You should remove this winter mulch in spring as the irises begin to grow and use the material later to refresh the summer mulch, which will break down rapidly in warm weather, when soil microbes are more active.

WAKING UP TO SPRING

The degree of winter dormancy shown by Louisiana Irises changes with climate and variety. Some kinds will show some green foliage all winter, which may be damaged by freezes, while others will lose all their leaves. Mild winter climates encourage growth, and only a short dormant spell occurs. In any case, new growth will appear early in spring.

If a heavy winter mulch was used, you should remove it as soon as the iris shoots emerge to avoid bleaching and weakening them. As the new leaves grow stronger, many experienced growers like to apply commercial fertilizers. The best recommendation seems to be an acidic azalea or camellia fertilizer, applied at a rate recommended by the packager. However, I have found that fertilization is not necessary for good bloom if a steady supply of organic matter is provided in the form of mulch. I apply well-composted leaf mold in late fall, after cutting off any drooping or damaged iris leaves (just for convenience). Northern growers who have only a short season in which to mature rhizomes might find some advantage in forcing them along with regular applications of granular or soluble fertilizers. In any case, use products recommended for acid-loving plants.

After-bloom care

Once the plants have bloomed, the iris bed should be kept well watered. If nature does not oblige, provide a good soaking at least once a week; if the bed can be flooded, so much the better. While growth naturally slows down in the summer, the plants should not be allowed to lose their leaves and go dormant. Louisiana Irises are favorites of bumblebees, and seed pods will form behind many of the flowers. Unless seeds are wanted for some reason, the old stalks should be cut off close to the rhizome. They generally cannot be pulled or broken off, and to try to do so may uproot the rhizome.

Dividing and Replanting

Louisiana Irises increase rapidly, with each old rhizome forming as many as a half-dozen offshoots along its length, and all of these may reach blooming size in a single season if cultural conditions are good. Late summer and early fall seem to be the best seasons for renovating plantings of these irises. Mature rhizomes may be up to 8 in. long, with numerous offsets along their length on either side.

Dig up the clump, following the general instructions for Siberian Irises on pp. 68-70. New, vigorous rhizomes can be cut from the older ones with a sharp knife or simply broken off. It is very important to have buckets of water handy into which the rhizomes can immediately be plunged. At no time should the roots be allowed to dry out.

After tilling additional organic matter into the bed, reset the divided plants immediately. Add new mulch and the job is done, except for close attention to watering, especially if dry weather occurs. You can give away any leftover plants or sell them for the benefit of local horticultural organizations. Or, as I do, you can play "Johnny Iris-seed" and stick the extras into the mud at the margins of local farm ponds, park pools, or even roadside ditches. I sometimes carry a few with me in a plastic bag on fishing trips to nearby ponds. Most will establish themselves and give pleasure to passersby in years to come.

Once they have bloomed, old rhizomes will not flower again, but they need not be discarded. You can use old, spent rhizomes to propagate new plants. Just plant each one in a large pot of rich soil and stand the pot in water (large plastic washtubs or dishpans work well). Soon, new shoots will emerge from dormant buds along the rhizome's length, and these may even reach blooming size by the following spring. After they have developed their own strong root systems, they can be planted in the garden.

Diseases and Pests

Louisiana Irises are largely free of diseases and pests, especially in their native haunts along the Gulf Coast. When grown in areas where conditions are less favorable, though, they may become more susceptible to disease. Most of the diseases of these irises can be avoided by good culture. Louisiana Irises that are grown in boggy places or in shallow water seem almost entirely immune to diseases and insect pests.

RHIZOME ROT

Rot in Louisiana Irises is usually caused by bacteria, and it is an occasional problem when these plants are grown under ordinary garden conditions. It can occur when the rhizomes are scalded by exposure to direct sunlight, so keeping a good mulch over the irises will do much to prevent it. If rot does occur, you can use a sharpened teaspoon to clean out the rotted material back to crisp white or pink tissue. Dust the wound with horticultural sulfur.

IRIS RUST

The only significant foliage problem for Louisiana Irises is iris rust, a fungal disease that produces small, rusty-colored pustules on the surfaces of the leaves. Plants are damaged when a good deal of leaf area is lost. The causative organism, *Puccinia iridis*, is related to rusts that attack other plants, such as wheat or barley, but not much is known about it. Systemic fungicides may be effective, but the best strategy is to limit the infection by cutting off any affected leaves as soon as the disease is noticed. Cleaning up and burning old foliage also help.

LEAF MINERS

Leaf miners may attack Louisiana Irises, but almost never go for other irises. Small white channels appear in the leaves, mostly toward the bases. If these attacked leaves are assiduously removed, the insects will gradually disappear. For severe infestations, an early spray with a systemic insecticide will be effective; contact insecticides are useless since the insects are already inside the leaves.

IRIS BORERS

Iris borers cannot attack the rhizomes of Louisiana Irises grown in water. The most favorable regions for growing Louisiana Irises are also far to the south of the borer's range. However, when these irises are grown in garden beds within regions where borers are known to occur, borers can indeed be a problem. In central Virginia, these large pink caterpillars with dark brown heads appear only every few years, but the last infestation in my garden focused on Louisiana Irises. As you would with Tall Bearded Irises, look for notches on the leaves near the center of the fan or obviously dying center leaves that pull away easily. If the borer has not reached the rhizome, it can often be crushed by pinching near the base of the fan, but if the rhizome has been invaded, it must be dug up and the culprit surgically removed.

As always, prevention is the best cure. In the fall, clean up and burn all old iris foliage, since that's where borer moths lay their eggs. Some growers recommend a routine spraying with a systemic insecticide when the iris fans are about 6 in. tall, and another just as bloomstalks are emerging. This is necessary only if there is a serious infestation. Iris borers are discussed in detail on pp. 54-57.

SLUGS AND SNAILS

Because Louisiana Irises are often grown in damp areas, snails and slugs can cause problems, actually feeding on the leaves and rhizomes by rasping the tissue with their tongues. Hand picking, baiting with shallow dishes of beer, and the use of a commercial slug bait are all effective. Use care with baits, however; some are attractive to pets and can be fatal to them.

VERTEBRATE PESTS

Mice, voles, deer, and rabbits are not usual pests of other irises, but they seem to like Louisianas. If the ground is relatively dry, mice and voles can tunnel under winter mulch and gnaw on rhizomes, even destroying them. This cannot happen if the plants are grown in shallow water and is unlikely to happen in a bog.

For mice and voles, there is no better solution than a garden cat, though one must be prepared also to lose the occasional songbird. Snap traps seem to catch few mice outdoors, and the more humane box traps are equally ineffective in a garden setting. (The latter leave you with the problem of what to do with the captured mice as well.) Poison baits designed to kill mice will also kill pets and other non-targeted animals that eat the attractive morsels. Better stick with the cat!

Deer and rabbits feed on foliage, usually in the early spring when little else is available. For deer and rabbits, I have found dried blood dust to be a very effective repellent. Most nurseries and garden centers sell this product in small bags; I get by on about 3 lb. a year, and it protects not only Louisiana Irises, but also tulips, pansies, alstroemerias, columbines, and other favorites. Evidently animal blood (this commercial form is a byproduct of the meat industry) contains chemicals that trigger an instinctive alarm reaction in rabbits and deer, and also renders treated foliage unpalatable. The light dusting of powdered dried blood needs to be reapplied after each rain.

Another good deer and rabbit repellent can be concocted from a couple of raw eggs, some crushed garlic cloves, and a teaspoon each of tabasco sauce and liquid detergent mixed in a gallon or two of water; spray it on plants that might be eaten. The odor cannot be detected by humans after the spray dries, but is extremely noxious to rabbits and deer.

IRISES FROM BULBS

The bulbous irises have never enjoyed much popularity with gardeners in North America. That may be because of their limited availability—almost all the average or beginning gardener can find in this line are inexpensive mixtures of Dutch Irises. As a result, many have never been able to sample the wonderful diversity of irises that grow from bulbs. These include not only the Dutch, Spanish, and English Irises (collectively called Xiphiums), perhaps the world's most popular cut flowers, but also the miniature, early-blooming Reticulatas and the strange Junos, which look like small corn plants bearing iris flowers. You may have to dig through catalogs to find them, but it will be worth the effort.

The bulbs of the three groups are easy to tell apart (photo, facing page). Those of the Junos (if they are healthy) bear thickened, fleshy roots. The Reticulatas lack these roots, and the bulbs are enclosed in a husk with a netted texture. Xiphium bulbs are similar to those of the Reticulatas, but are somewhat smaller and the husks are smooth.

Bulbs of bulbous irises. Top row, from left to right: the Juno *Iris bucharica*, with its characteristic fleshy roots; an English Iris; and the knobbly, root-like corm of *Hermodactylus tuberosus* (see the sidebar on p. 96). Bottom row, from left to right: Spanish, Dutch, and Reticulata Iris bulbs.

The Xiphiums

Probably more money is to be made growing Xiphium Irises than growing all other types combined. Vast numbers of bulbs are produced each year and sold to cut-flower growers, who let them bloom once and then discard them—they cost only pennies when purchased in thousands. By manipulating temperatures and dormancy, the bulbs can be brought into flower at any time of the year. The blooms, usually cut in the bud stage, can be stored for as long as a week in coolers, and open normally when warmed up. Order irises from a florist, and Xiphiums are what you get.

The seven or eight species in the group are all natives of the western Mediterranean: Spain, Portugal, Morocco, southern Italy, and Sicily, with one species extending north into the Pyrenees. These days the species are for the most part grown only by specialists and botanical gardens, having been supplanted by selections and hybrids. Today Xiphiums are classified, somewhat arbitrarily, into Spanish, Dutch, and English Irises.

SPANISH IRISES

Of the three groups of varieties, only the Spanish Irises are aptly named. They are all selections from the single species *Iris xiphium*, which is indeed native to Spain (as well as France, Italy, and North Africa). Spanish Irises come in a wide color range that reflects the variability of the parent species. Growing from small, hard bulbs with a tough tunic, or outer husk, varieties with white, violet, red-purple, blue, and yellow flowers are available. All have rather grassy, rush-like foliage.

Spanish Irises have flowers from 3 in. to 4 in. wide, held on stems that may reach a length of 18 in. They have the insouciant charm of plants that retain the characters of the wild species from which they sprang. Their bloom season usually coincides with the Tall Bearded Iris season.

DUTCH IRISES

Their name notwithstanding, Dutch Irises are not native to the Low Countries, but are the product of the Dutch genius for flower breeding and selection. They are the results of crosses between selected varieties of Spanish Irises (*I. xiphium*) and some of the other Xiphium species, such as *I. tingitana, I. fontanesii,* and *I. filifolia.* The resulting plants were then crossed among themselves for many generations and selected for larger flowers and taller stems.

Today's varieties are far removed from the parent species, though the hybridizing work began as recently as the early years of this century. With 4-in. to 5-in. flowers on 2-ft. stems, the Dutch Irises (photo, below left) have the same wide color range as the Spanish Irises, and their hybrid background gives them great vigor. Because they include genes from the early-blooming *I. xiphium praecox,* they flower about two weeks earlier than the Spanish Irises and are good companions for late tulips (Dutch iris with too much *praecox* in them may develop too rapidly in spring and get nipped by late

'White Perfection' is an excellent example of a Dutch hybrid iris.

English irises descend from *Iris latifolia,* which is native to the Pyrenees Mountains, between Spain and France.

freezes; this is unfortunately true of the lovely old blue 'Wedgewood'). It is these irises that are grown in such huge numbers for the cut-flower trade.

ENGLISH IRISES

English Irises are no more English than the Dutch Irises are Dutch. These are all selections from the species *Iris latifolia* (photo at right, facing page), the Xiphium species of the Pyrenees. Their name comes from the fact that they first became popular in England, and the named varieties were raised there. The bulbs are rather fragile, and the flowers are broader and more opulent than their those of their southern cousins, typically 5 in. wide and held on 2-ft. to 3-ft. stems. Their foliage is broader and less grassy and rush-like. English Irises have a more limited color range than the Dutch and Spanish strains; you'll find lovely whites to deep red-purples, passing through all shades between, as well as fine, clear blues. Their blooming season is later than even the Spanish Irises, and they span the brief gap between the Tall Bearded Irises and the Japanese Irises.

Growing Xiphium Irises

If you want to try your hand at growing Xiphiums, you might have a little trouble finding interesting varieties. The bulbs of the Dutch Irises can be easily obtained; nearly every general mail-order catalog or bulb house has them, and they are a staple in the bulb bins at garden centers in the fall. Unfortunately, these are usually mixtures, or only a few older varieties are singled out. The prices, especially by mail, are extraordinarily cheap when the bulbs are purchased in lots of 50 or more. Spanish and English Irises are a bit more difficult to find. All three are sold as dry bulbs, available in the fall, but I have noticed that some local stores offer them prepackaged for sale in the spring. Spring planting won't work (see p. 92), so resist the temptation.

Xiphiums are easily grown with an understanding that the English Irises have quite different requirements from the Spanish and Dutch varieties. Let's look at the latter first.

CULTURAL REQUIREMENTS FOR SPANISH AND DUTCH IRISES

Spanish and Dutch Irises require essentially the same cultural conditions. The species from which they were derived are native to Mediterranean climates, with cool, moist winters and hot, dry summers. Accordingly, these irises do most of their growing in the winter (where possible) and spring. Then they relish a good baking through the summer, to be revived by autumn rains.

Given this background, they are surprisingly hardy (at least into USDA Zone 6, and Zone 5 with some winter protection) and tolerant of summer moisture. But to turn them into true perennials, they need the summer drying-off. In gardens with cold, snowy winters and wet summers they will persist only for a season or two before dwindling away. Spanish and Dutch Irises prefer a lighter soil texture to clay, They are not fond of too much organic matter, but they do appreciate a good bit of lime.

Planting the bulbs

Spanish and Dutch Iris bulbs are available, packed dry, in the fall along with the other "Dutch" bulbs. Fall planting is the only road to success. Planting these bulbs in the spring won't work, since the weather warms too quickly for them to establish an adequate root system to support the foliage and flower stems.

Exactly when to plant in the fall depends somewhat on experience. In the South (Zones 7 and 8), early planting (late September) succeeds best, while north of Zone 7, later planting (October through November) works better. The reason is the tendency of the bulbs to put up foliage shortly after planting. Exposed to the rigors of a northern winter, this foliage will be damaged, and the plants themselves may be killed; by planting late the chances of this happening are minimized. Early planting in the South allows foliage development, which will survive the mild winter and get the plants off to a quicker start in the spring. Wherever or whenever, put the bulbs down about 4 in.

Seasonal care

Fertilization is not required with Spanish and Dutch Irises, which favor lean soil. Their extensive root systems reach far and wide to seek out nutrients.

With the arrival of warm weather in the spring, the plants grow rapidly and soon the fat buds emerge from the narrow fans of grassy leaves. Each stem will carry two (rarely three) flowers, which bloom in succession. While they are the cut flower *par excellence*, their garden impact is also great, especially when closely planted in masses of the same variety.

After flowering, the foliage persists for a few weeks, building strength into the bulb for the next year's bloom. This old foliage should not be removed until it has thoroughly withered. Then it will come away with a sharp tug.

In climates that suit them, Dutch and Spanish Irises can be left in the ground over summer and will increase from small bulblets that form around the old ones. These bulblets take a second year of growth to reach blooming size. But under conditions such as those here in central Virginia, most of the bulbs will succumb during the summer, and only a few will return for a second year of bloom. (Of all the ones I planted, the only ones that lived to bloom a second time were a few I luckily placed on a gravelly ridge—these bloomed and increased for several years, probably because of the excellent drainage.)

The bulbs are so inexpensive that they can be treated like annuals and replanted each fall from fresh stock, but if you are particularly fond of a hard-to-get variety or just naturally frugal, Dutch and Spanish Irises can be dug up after the leaves have gone and stored dry (in sand or vermiculite) in a warm place until fall. You can remove the small bulblets and grow them on in a nursery bed until they reach blooming size.

CULTURAL REQUIREMENTS
FOR ENGLISH IRISES

English Irises require a completely different regimen from the one just described. They hail from moist mountain meadows in the Pyrenees, and while as hardy as or hardier than the Spanish and Dutch Irises, they are also entirely tolerant of summer moisture. Perhaps this explains their popularity in England!

Summer heat, however, is to be avoided. English Irises do not succeed where summers are hot; I have not been able to grow them here in Zone 7a, but they should be tried in the Appalachian mountains, where summers are naturally cooler. The Pacific Northwest provides the ideal conditions for these irises, but they have also succeeded in southern New England, upstate New York, and the cooler elevations of the southern Appalachian Mountains. Unfortunately, most stocks are virus infected and show dark streaks in the flowers. The virus seems not to harm the plants' vigor, however. Plants grown from seed and kept isolated from infected ones are virus free.

With English Irises, a cool, fluffy, humus-rich soil with some lime added works best. Handle the bulbs with care—they lack the coarse husks of the Spanish and Dutch Irises and are easily bruised. Plant in the fall, about 6 in. deep.

The English Irises do not make winter foliage and get off to a late start in the spring, and it is well to mark where they were planted so they do not get beheaded by cultivation or weeding. The broad, channeled foliage and flowering stems will reach a height of 2 ft., sometimes 3 ft., and each stem will carry two flowers. For home use as cut flowers, they are superb.

It is not necessary to dig the bulbs up if they seem happy where they are; they will slowly form compact groups (photo, above right). A recent trip to Scotland in late June was highlighted by unforgettable clumps of these irises in roadside cottage gardens.

These English irises are very much at home in a garden in southern Scotland. The size of the clump suggests that they have not been divided or moved for many years, and the lack of virus streaking indicates an origin from local seed.

The Reticulatas

When I examine my collection of slides and photographs of flowers, I'm often surprised by how many pictures I have of *Hepatica,* the earliest-blooming wildflower in my region, and of various kinds of crocuses. I finally decided that this was a perfectly normal reaction: after the long, cold winter we really need flowers, and photographers respond by shooting rolls and rolls of film! Thus the plants that dare to poke their blooming heads above the melting snow are especially precious. Those of us who are iris enthusiasts are very lucky that we don't have to wait long at all to have irises blooming in our garden; the Reticulata Irises are there with the earliest crocuses.

THE BULB FRAME

Junos (see pp. 97-100) and Aril Irises (see pp. 127-133) are difficult for the average gardener to grow because they require a long period of warm, dry curing during their summer dormant period. Any rain during this time is likely to cause them to rot. In addition, a number of species begin to grow in the early winter, producing foliage that is susceptible to freeze damage; still others are not fully hardy.

A solution available to the enthusiast for these irises is the bulb frame (photo, below right). Popular with British gardeners, bulb frames are constructions within which conditions can be controlled to a much greater extent than in the open ground. The bulb frame is nothing more than a raised bed covered with a frame that supports panes of glass, fiberglass, or plastic. The fundamental idea is to be able to provide protection from both winter cold and summer wetness.

Bulb frames can be constructed to almost any dimensions, and a variety of materials can be used, including rot-resistant lumber, railroad ties, landscaping timbers, brick, and concrete block. If only a modest number of plants is to be grown, you might start with a base about 4 ft. by 6 ft. that is 2 ft. to 3 ft. high. (If you plan to use a prefabricated cold frame on top, just design the base accordingly.) The frame should be sited either on a south-facing slope or against a wall that faces south or southeast. Low spots are to be avoided, since it is important that water be able to drain away from the frame.

The top of the frame is to be furnished with slanting panes of glass or plastic, arranged so as to accommodate the height of the plants to be grown. It should be possible to lift the panes easily to provide ventilation on warm days in spring. The function of the panes is to keep off summer rain and to increase the temperature inside the frame to simulate the desert climate that Junos and Arils love.

Fill the bottom several inches of the base with coarse gravel to facilitate drainage. You may also want to make openings in the first course of blocks or timbers to allow water to run out freely—especially if the soil beneath is clay. Place a screen of heavy-gauge hardware cloth over the gravel layer to separate it from the soil mix. Now fill up the frame with a quick-draining soil mix containing pea gravel, small volcanic cinders, or some other material to facilitate the passage of water. Some water retention will be required, so use a generous proportion of organic matter. Because the amount of soil in the frame is limited and probably will not be replaced very often, you'll have to use artificial fertilizers to provide the nutrition needed by the plants, especially after the first few years.

The irises are planted in the frame at the usual time, and watered. Since the objective is to control the amount of water received by the plants, all watering should be done by hand. (You might want to run a pipe or hose to a fixture attached to the side of the frame to make this task easier.) Through the fall and winter, keep the soil just moist. You can give more water in the spring and continue to do so until after the plants bloom, when water should be gradually witheld until the plants are completely dry and dormant. Keep the panes closed on most days, opening them for ventilation only if temperatures get too hot or if humidity is high. Many manufactured cold frames come with automatic venting systems that can handle this for you.

Bulb frames are used with great success in the Royal Botanical Gardens at Kew and Edinburgh. I've seen both Junos and Aril Irises blooming beautifully at Kew, while outside the bulb frames, cold English rain fell.

This bulb frame at Kew Gardens in England is used to grow an extensive collection of Juno iris species.

The Reticulatas are a group of ten or a dozen species spread through the western Mediterranean from Israel through Turkey and into Iran and Central Asia. Like the Xiphiums, they enjoy hot, dry summers, but at least one or two of them easily adapt to the wetter summers found in most of our gardens. These species make excellent rock-garden plants, enjoying the perfect drainage they find there and well in keeping with other diminutive plants. Collectors who want to grow the more finicky species use a bulb frame (see the sidebar on the facing page).

The typical Reticulata Iris is *Iris reticulata* (photo, top right). Only 3 in. to 4 in. tall at blooming time, it produces a single, deep red-purple flower that looks like a somewhat attenuated version of a Dutch Iris. Large for the height of its stem, this flower is as much as 2 in. across and may have a delightful scent, which you'll miss unless you get down on your knees and bend close to the blossom. The narrow leaves, which may be a few inches taller than the flowering stem, are square in cross section, like a mint stem; later they grow as much as 1 ft. tall before withering in early summer. One has to be careful not to pull them off before they mature, since their grassy appearance mimics some weed grasses.

Iris histrioides is a slightly larger Reticulata Iris, usually with bluer flowers having a variable degree of darker spotting on the falls and with a bright yellow, smooth crest. Most of the named varieties available are selections from this species or hybrids having it as one parent. The yellow note is sounded by *I. danfordiae*, (photo, bottom right). It is somewhat more petite than either of the two previously mentioned species, but otherwise similar in form.

Iris reticulata blooms with the crocuses. Some varieties and hybrids are intensely fragrant.

Iris danfordiae, a yellow-flowered Reticulata Iris.

GROWING RETICULATA IRISES

Reticulatas are usually available from general bulb dealers as mixtures, but my experience has been that not much variety is supplied—nearly all the flowers will be either some shade of purple or violet-blue, and despite the photographs accompanying the descriptions, white and yellow forms are not included. To get the yellow, you must buy *I. danfordiae* under its own name.

Specialists or larger mail-order firms will sometimes offer the newer hybrid varieties with larger, broader flowers, such as 'Joyce' and 'George', which are well worth having. 'Katherine Hodgkin', a hybrid between *I. histrioides* and the exceedingly rare *I. winowgradowii,* though first grown years ago, is just now appearing in some catalogs. It has beautiful, very full flowers of pale yellow veined and washed in sky blue.

AN IRIS IMPERSONATOR

The Snake's Head Iris *(Hermodactylus tuberosus)* is the only species of its genus, a genus evidently closely related to *Iris,* with flowers that fit the typical iris pattern. In fact, in both flowers and foliage, it closely resembles a Reticulata Iris. Look at its underground parts, though, and the similarities disappear. This iris impersonator grows 4 in. to 6 in. tall from small, thick yet brittle dahlia-like tubers. The color of the bloom is also unusual (photo, right). It's apple green, with a blackish purple spot on each fall petal. The English name is hard to account for, but perhaps the emerging flower buds do look a little like a snake's head.

Common around the Mediterranean from France to Israel, the Snake's Head Iris is an early bloomer, following hard on the heels of the Reticulata Irises and in company with the Miniature Dwarf Bearded Hybrids. The tubers are sometimes available from mail-order bulb dealers and are usually quite

***Hermodactylus tuberosus,* the Snake's Head Iris.**

inexpensive. They should be planted a few inches deep. Alkaline to neutral soils are best, and go easy on the organic matter. A fertile sandy loam gives good results.

Like most Mediterranean plants, the Snake's Head Iris likes dry heat in the summer and quickly multiplies when planted against walls, which reflect heat and also provide some protection from summer rains. Container culture, much as outlined for the Juno Irises on pp. 99-100, is another way to succeed with the Snake's Head Iris, and I suspect this plant might soon take over a bulb frame!

Hardiness is a question. German expert Fritz Köhlein suspects that the Snake's Head Iris is not fully hardy in northern climates and recommends container culture, so the pots can be sheltered from frost. However, I've grown this unusual plant outside in the mountains of northern Pennsylvania, where winter temperatures regularly drop well below 0°F. It even flowered! Admittedly it was at the base of a south-facing foundation, but I think *Hermodactylus* might be hardier than generally thought.

The small bulbs are shipped dry in the fall. Reticulata bulbs are immediately recognizable by their husks, or tunics, which are peculiarly netted with strong fibers running at angles to one another. Since these bulbs do not make winter foliage, they can be planted as early as September.

Plant the bulbs about 4 in. to 5 in. deep. Deep planting is recommended for Reticulata Irises, since a number of the species and varieties tend to "break up" into many small bulblets after the first season. *Iris danfordiae* is particularly prone to do this. Somehow the deeper planting prevents it, but no one knows just why.

Like other bulbous irises, Reticulatas favor light soils, so heavy clay should be amended with coarse sand or chicken grit. Too much organic matter can lead to disease in these bulbs, and excess fertility causes them to run mostly to leaves and small bulblets at the expense of flowers. Ground limestone is a good additive if your soil is naturally acid.

Foliage will emerge very early—late January in my USDA Zone 7a garden—followed by flowers at the first hint of warm weather. Both the leaves and flowers seem immune to late frosts and freezes. After the plant blooms, the foliage continues to grow for a time and should be allowed to mature naturally, in order to build the strength of the bulbs for next season. If in spite of your best efforts you find that these tiny treasures dwindle away in a few seasons, they are inexpensive and worth replacing, even on an annual basis. However, in climates where summers are too wet, the bulbs can be lifted and stored as recommended on p. 92 for Dutch Irises.

The Junos

Juno Irises are the most un-iris like of all the plants discussed in this book. Botanists have debated for decades over the proper name for this group—are they really *Iris,* or do they belong in their own distinct genus, *Juno?* The confusion is furthered by the availability of still another name, *Scorpiris,* which is also used for these strange plants. Whatever the case, it would be a severe loss to the genus *Iris* if they were removed; about one-third of all described *Iris* species belong in this group. Of all these, though, only three species in the group are at all readily available. The most common of these is *Iris bucharica.*

Iris bucharica is a native of southern Russia and Afghanistan that grows in rough, mountainous country. Like all Junos, the modest-sized, pear-shaped bulb has growing from its base thickened storage roots that somewhat resemble the roots of a daylily plant. As the plants grow in spring, the food stored in these roots is withdrawn, and a new set of roots starts to grow.

Above ground, the glossy, rich green leaves of Junos are carried on an elongating stem, giving the appearance of a miniature corn plant (bottom photo, p. 98). Flowers are produced in the leaf axils, and the top bud blooms first, with those lower down following. As many as six or eight flowers will appear on really well-grown plants. They are in various shades of yellow, but the most common form has white standards and style arms, with butter-yellow falls. The standards are small (and in many

Iris bucharica is the most readily available and most easily grown Juno Iris.

Iris magnifica.

Junos nonexistent), but are made up for by the large style arms. Lately, *I. bucharica* has been appearing in the catalogs of the larger bulb-selling firms.

Less readily available is *Iris magnifica*, a plant that grows to 2 ft. tall, but with the same corn-like form as *bucharica*. From Central Asia, near fabled Samarkand, it produces four or five large, lilac-blue flowers (photo, below left).

From Turkey and Iran comes *Iris aucheri*, another tall Juno with clear blue flowers. This species has been known in the past as *I. sindjarensis,* and with the rare and difficult *I. persica* is the parent of one of the few named hybrid Junos, 'Sindpers'.

GROWING JUNO IRISES

Despite the many named species, Junos are rare in most North American and European gardens. It's a combination of very limited availability and difficult culture, plus the fact that a good number of the species are simply not attractive enough to make garden plants. However, this group is a collector's paradise, offering variety in abundance and a real challenge to the gardener's skill.

Iris bucharica, I. magnifica, and *I. aucheri* can easily be grown in the open if some attention is paid to their needs. Juno Irises hail from regions where winters are often long and snowy. In spring, abundant moisture is available from the melting snow, and the plants grow and flower with almost incredible speed. The summer that quickly follows the wet spring is often hot and dry, and the plants must use this short window of opportunity to flower, mature seed, and store food in the bulb and roots for the next season's bloom.

In their native habitat, these three species often grow on slopes, amongst rocks or in scree (scree is the deep debris of broken and shattered rock that slides from cliffs and steep mountainsides). There are exceptions—bulb expert Brian Mathew published a photograph of *Iris aucheri* growing on flat ground around the margins of a temporary pond in Turkey.

JUNOS IN OPEN GROUND

The following outdoor cultural advice applies to *I. bucharica, I. magnifica,* and *I. aucheri;* for the other, rarer species, the best strategy is either container culture (see the next section) or a bulb frame (see the sidebar on p. 94). Bulbs will be shipped dry in autumn. Check them carefully; if the swollen storage roots are missing, most authorities say that the bulbs will have a difficult time establishing themselves (other growers claim that it makes no real difference and enough food is stored in the bulb to get the plants off to a good start).

Select a well-drained site with light-textured soil; some fine gravel or chicken grit can be mixed in (and if this latter is of ground limestone, so much the better, since Junos prefer alkaline soils). Clay soils or those with a great deal of organic matter are dangerous for Junos, which require rapid drainage and are susceptible to a variety of bulb rot diseases.

Plant your bulbs at a depth about two to three times their height, with the storage roots carefully spread out. Backfill the holes carefully to prevent damage to the bulb or its roots.

Since some Junos have a tendency to grow in winter, it's a good idea to protect the planting site against winter moisture by covering it with plastic or an old window sash. The protection is needed because this winter foliage may be damaged by hard freezes. Later in the spring, if the weather is threatening, the plants can be protected by old boxes turned over them. This is more effective if two boxes, a small one over the plants and a larger one over the smaller, are used. The layer of still air trapped between the two boxes is an effective insulator.

When the weather first warms in spring, remove the protection and allow spring rains to soak in. At this time, some authorities recommend scattering a slow-release granular fertilizer over the surface of the soil. Rains will carry the nutrients down to the roots; such fertilization may be beneficial because Junos have a relatively short period of growth.

After the plants bloom, allow the foliage to mature fully. If the planting site is well drained or if the summers in your region are naturally hot and dry, the bulbs can be left in place to increase (which *I. bucharica,* in particular, does quite rapidly) and form attractive clumps. If nature does not cooperate, you can dig up the bulbs—again, be careful of those storage roots— and store them in a warm place in dry sand or vermiculite until you are ready to replant them in the fall.

JUNOS IN CONTAINERS

Container culture bypasses the pitfalls of growing Junos in the open (mainly summer moisture) and may be the only way of handling the rarer species.

A collection of Reticulata Iris species and varieties blooming in pots.

When I visited Kew Gardens, near London, in April of 1996, it was exciting to see a number of exotic Juno species blooming in pots outside the alpine houses (unheated greenhouses). Rather large, deep pots for the expected size of the plant were being used, since deep pots provide better drainage and the Juno Irises have extensive, vigorous root systems.

The best soil mix for Juno Irises incorporates lots of coarse drainage material, such as grit, ground volcanic cinders, or perlite. For the most delicate species, the lower half of the pot may be filled with coarser gravel. After potting in the fall about 1 in. deep, the bulbs should be lightly watered and stored in a cool place; the hardier species can be left outside so long as there is some protection against actual freezing and excess moisture. Some growth may occur in winter.

In late winter or early spring, abundant water should be given while the plants grow and bloom. In the summer, the bulbs are dried off until repotting time in the fall. Bulb-frame culture is even easier, since the frame keeps off winter wet and also warms the soil. Even difficult species may form good clumps in a bulb frame, according to Brian Mathew.

PROPAGATION

Propagation of Junos is a tricky matter. The three easy species (*bucharica, magnifica,* and *aucheri*) increase well left on their own from small bulblets that develop around the base or from the natural division of large bulbs. Bulbs separated from a clump may be injured slightly and thus become susceptible to rot.

If storage roots are broken off, they may produce new bulbs if a fragment of the basal plate (stem) of the bulb is attached, but they are also likely to decay if there is too much moisture.

Diseases and Pests of Bulbous Irises

With the exception of English Irises, which prefer a moist, organic soil, nearly all disease problems with bulbous irises are associated with poorly drained or excessively organic soils. Under these conditions, several bulb rots may attack and decimate plantings. Control is difficult; usually affected plants have to be destroyed.

PENICILLIUM ROT

Purchased bulbs need to be carefully scrutinized for *Penicillium* rot, which appears as a grayish or bluish, sometimes furry patch on the bulb. If present, this fungus will destroy the infected bulb after planting, then spread to other bulbs. Reject infected bulbs; do not purchase any in which the tunics, or husks, have been pulled off.

SCLEROTIUM ROT

Sclerotium rot in bulbous irises is a different species of fungus than the one that causes a similar disease in rhizomatous irises; this one also attacks tulips, lilies, and other bulbs. On a plant infected with sclerotium rot, you will see a white, netted growth at the base of the leaves and over the bulb. Unless the plant is particularly valuable, it is best to remove it and destroy it, along with much of the surrounding soil. Bulbs that you absolutely must save can be dug, washed, and soaked for an hour in a solution of systemic fungicide before being replanted in a pot or in another spot where there is no evidence of disease.

INK-SPOT DISEASE

Ink-spot disease most often affects Reticulata Irises, and it can spread rapidly. Infected bulbs show the black spots that gives the disease its name, and the plant will rapidly succumb. Brian Mathew reports success in controlling it with systemic fungicides, both as a dip before planting and as a solution poured heavily around the plants. Since fungi are so troublesome for these irises, a preplanting treatment of the bulbs with fungicide would probably be a wise preventive measure.

APHIDS

Aphids (greenflies) are probably the only serious insect pests of bulbous irises, but because the plants grow so rapidly, these insects rarely have time to build up harmful populations. However, aphids spread viruses and so should be dealt with when they appear, as the virus infections are incurable and weaken the plants as well as mar the flowers.

While present in low numbers, aphids can simply be brushed off plants. If the infestation grows worse, insecticidal soap is best for use on foliage. When iris bulbs are in storage they can be lightly dusted with a powdered insecticide to prevent aphids from colonizing the bulbs.

IRISES FOR THE WATERSIDE

This chapter discusses a group of irises that are usually associated with water gardens, though most (if not all) of them can be grown in ordinary garden beds with some added attention to watering and culture. Among them are the well-known Japanese Irises (top photo, facing page), hybrids based on the species *Iris ensata. Iris laevigata,* also found in east Asia, the widespread *I. pseudacorus,* and the North American species *I. versicolor* and *I. virginica* also belong in this grouping. When held up to the light, the leaves of some of these irises show, in addition to the parallel longitudinal veins, short, horizontal cross-veins called "water marks," a sure indication of a water-loving iris (see the photo at left on p. 76).

Japanese Irises

When gardeners think about Japanese culture, they think of Japanese Irises. For nearly a century, these irises have also been popular with Americans who appreciate their spectacular beauty and intriguing history.

Japanese Irises sparkle along the waterside, their natural element.

At least 800 years ago, Japanese gardeners began collecting plants of *Iris ensata* from the wild, giving them the common name Hana-ayame (photo, right). Struck by the variation that occurred within this single species, they first selected and later deliberately bred hundreds of varieties. As the centuries passed, appreciation of these irises increased, until, in the early 19th century, Sadamoto Matsudaira, following in the footsteps of his father, began a program of intensive development that brought these irises to the apex of perfection. Sadamoto later adopted the name Sho-o, or "old man of the irises," and helped popularize the Japanese name used for these irises today, Hanashobu. Sho-o produced not only single varieties (with typical iris form, bearing upright standards and reflexed falls) but also so-called doubles, in

Iris ensata, native to Japan and northeastern Asia, is the progenitor of the many varieties of Japanese Iris.

which the standards are replaced by a second set of falls. He regarded as his supreme achievement a variety with many extra petals, resembling a peony (these true doubles are rarely grown today).

In his delightful book on Japanese Irises (see p. 167), Currier McEwen describes how contemporaries and followers of Sho-o originated new strains and entered into fierce competition with one another to grow the very best irises. Prized varieties were jealously guarded and often not shared outside the family. The story reads like a more refined, Japanese version of the "tulipomania" that had seized the Netherlands almost two centuries earlier!

Japanese Irises came to the United States in the years following the Civil War, as Japan was gradually opened to commerce and cultural contact with the West. American growers were intrigued by the exotic appearance of the Japanese Irises and began their own breeding programs, introducing varieties better adapted to American conditions. But after an initial period of great popularity, interest seemed to decline, probably—according to Dr. McEwen— because of a lack of understanding of how to grow them properly. The publication of his book in 1990 is an indication of the comeback now being staged by Japanese Irises in the United States, and a number of speciality nurseries, some with color catalogs, have emerged (see pp. 162-165). The latest developments have included the appearance of colchicine-induced tetraploids, repeat-blooming varieties, and the production of fertile hybrids with *Iris pseudacorus,* introducing yellow into the Japanese Iris spectrum for the first time.

THE PLANTS

Japanese Irises grow from finger-shaped, fiber-covered rhizomes, which, rather than creeping along the surface of the ground, grow in a more upright position. The fans of sturdy foliage can easily be distinguished from most other irises, since each leaf has a prominent midrib, or large central vein, which helps to support and stiffen it. Flowering stems 2 ft. to 4 ft. tall rise above the foliage and usually have at least one branch. Up to three branches may be present in some of the latest American varieties.

THE FLOWERS

The flowers of some Japanese Irises are the largest known of any irises, reaching 10 in. or more in diameter (about the size of a common dinner plate), but most are from 6 in. to 8 in. across . Flowers may be singles or doubles. Singles (top left photo, facing page) are flowers with the typical upright standards found in other iris types; the standards are usually a good deal smaller than the falls and because of this, singles are often called "three-petaled" flowers.

In doubles, on the other hand, the standards are replaced by a second set of falls, producing "six-petaled" blooms (top right photo, facing page). The most desirable form in both of these types is flaring to horizontal, making the blooms most attractive when viewed from above, as from a bridge or river bank. In some varieties, still more petals appear, some derived from stamens and style arms, culminating in Sho-o's treasured peony form (bottom photo, facing page).

'Summer Splash' is a single, or three-petaled, Japanese Iris with uncommonly graceful form.

This unnamed seedling exemplifies the opulent double, or six-petaled, Japanese Irises.

Color and pattern

The color range of Japanese Irises has traditionally been somewhat limited, since all varieties are derived from just a single species, whose color in nature ranges from pale lavender to a deep reddish purple. Breeders have succeeded in producing near pinks and almost true blues to add to the violet hues. Pristine whites are now available (top photo, p. 106), and recent hybrids with *Iris pseudacorus* have added yellows (these are not yet very widely available and are rather weak growers).

However, the limited color range is more than made up for by an incredible array of patterns. Selfs and bitones occur, including amoenas with white standards and colored falls, and reverse bitones with darkly pigmented standards over lighter falls. In addition, color may be applied to the petals in a number of ways, including veined patterns as well as brushed and sanded ones, in which the pigment is in the form of minute dots either evenly scattered or streaked on the lighter surfaces of the petals.

'Rose Adagio' comes close to Sho-o's ideal of a peony-like Japanese Iris bloom.

Pure white Japanese Irises glow against dark foliage. This is an unnamed seedling in the author's garden.

'Persephone' combines a rich red-violet base color with a striking lined pattern in white.

A particularly delightful pattern is referred to as "lined," in which the dark ground color of the falls contrasts with broad white lines following the veins after emerging from a white central area (photo, below left). Color can also appear on the petals in no coherent pattern at all, but splashed and dappled irregularly (top left photo, facing page). Contrasting edgings of either a lighter or darker color are a feature of many newer hybrids (top right photo, facing page).

Bloom season

Japanese irises bloom much later than the Tall Bearded hybrids, and there is usually no overlap at all in their blooming seasons. In my central Virginia garden, the Japanese Irises are a main feature of the June border (bottom photo, facing page), combining beautifully with lilies and hemerocallis. Farther north, New Englanders report that the flowering of some Japanese Iris varieties extends to August or even on into September! With proper selection of varieties, about six weeks of bloom can be attained.

Within the last two decades, varieties of Japanese Irises have appeared that show both continuing bloom and repeat bloom. The continuing bloomers have rhizomes that mature at different rates and thus send up from a clump a succession of stalks for up to a month or more, while the repeat bloomers provide a second season after a short rest. Currier McEwen has reported on seedlings that not only repeat, but also rebloom in the fall after the fashion of some of the Tall Bearded Irises (see the sidebar on p. 33). Few varieties with these characteristics have reached the public as yet, but they seem destined for immense popularity.

'Frilled Enchantment' (above) features abundant ruffles and a contrasting edging.

'Grape Fizz' (left) is a six-petaled Japanese Iris with deep purple flowers splashed in white.

Japanese Iris in a garden setting. Asiatic hybrid lilies in the background provide contrast.

IRIS SETOSA AND THE ICE AGES

Iris setosa, while not a member of the Laevigata-Water Iris group, would seem to be related since it crosses easily with them. Of all these irises, it is perhaps the least dependent on wet conditions and has one of the widest natural distributions of any iris species: from eastern Siberia through to Japan, and crossing the Bering Strait to Alaska. It's Alaska's only native iris. Absent from the center of the continent, it crops up again in eastern Canada and Maine, where some consider it a separate species *(I. hookeri).*

Botanists believe that *Iris setosa* once flourished across the Bering land bridge and throughout North America, but that the advance of the ice caps hundreds of thousands of years ago obliterated it in the middle part of the continent. Then, with the flooding of the Bering land bridge to create the Bering Strait, the Asian populations were separated from the Alaskan ones.

The flowers are a bit curious in the extreme reduction of the standard petals down to a small, hair-like filament that is not at all conspicuous (photo, right). Because the standards seem absent to the casual viewer, the series to which the species belongs is called Tripetalae. Colors vary from a rare pure white to deep blue-purples. The Alaskan variety is often less than 1 ft. tall; Asian and eastern Canadian forms are about twice as high, producing many flowers on branched stems.

Iris setosa **has the widest natural range of any iris species, from Siberia to eastern Canada. It's also a fine garden plant.**

A fine garden plant in its own right, *I. setosa* is in some ways a hybridizer's dream, because it can be crossed with so many other species, including the Laevigata group. *Iris setosa,* with *I. virginica,* is thought to be a parent of a third species, *I. versicolor.* The "marriage" seems to have happened when the glaciers were at their maximum extent and *I. setosa,* fleeing the icy conditions, moved south into the range of *virginica.* Later, as the ice retreated, *setosa* likewise crept back north, leaving its offspring *versicolor* behind. It also has been crossed with Siberian Irises ('Sibtosa' hybrids), and Pacific Coast Native Irises ('Tenosas').

Grow *I. setosa* in full sun in a moist, organic-rich soil, and treat it as you would a garden Siberian (see pp. 63-68). The dwarf forms are the hardiest, easily surviving in USDA Zone 3. *Iris tridentata,* an *I. setosa* relative, seems to require more moisture, and despite being native from North Carolina south into Florida, is hardy in gardens as far north as Ohio, Pennsylvania, and Massachusetts. This latter species has been virtually unused by breeders. It would be useful for its late-blooming qualities, flowering near the end of the Japanese Iris season.

Growing Japanese Irises

Japanese Irises are offered both by general nurseries and specialty gardens, some of which publish color catalogs. Plants obtained locally may be in containers—which is a really good thing if the containers have been kept standing in shallow water, but not so good if they have been left in the open nursery rows. With mail order you get bare-root rhizomes packed in wet peat and enclosed in plastic bags. It is very important that the roots not be allowed to dry out.

It's a misconception that Japanese Irises need to be in standing water to grow well—they're highly adaptable and can also thrive along the margins of a pond or stream, in a well-watered perennial border, or in containers, as long as their basic cultural requirements are met.

GENERAL CULTURAL REQUIREMENTS

The natural habitat of the parent species, *Iris ensata*, provides clues to good cultural practices for Japanese Irises. Found throughout Japan, in northern China, and in the Russian Far East, *I. ensata* is unquestionably hardy—some colonies withstand winter temperatures far below 0°F and deep snow cover for many months. Thus Japanese Irises should be well adapted to the northern United States and much of southern Canada.

Colonies of *Iris ensata* are usually found in open, grassy places that are low and boggy, with the acid, richly organic soil that typically occurs in such locales. Periodic spring flooding often deposits layers of new soil over the established plants, which they overcome by the partly vertical growth of their rhizomes. But sometimes the plants are found in standing water much of the year. The main period of active growth immediately follows blooming.

Given this knowledge, the ideal spot for Japanese Irises would seem to be along the waterside, especially on the borders of ponds or pools that are in the open. The soil should be rich in organic matter and on the acidic side.

Japanese Irises are undoubtedly best displayed as they are in Japan, in mass plantings dedicated to them alone. But gardeners all over the world have experimented with pushing these limits, and have found that Japanese Irises are surprisingly adaptable. With extra attention to watering, they thrive in borders alongside daylilies and other perennials. Though the best bloom is to be had from plants in full sunlight, they have proven remarkably tolerant of light shade, especially in the southern part of their range. And they are the best adapted of all irises to being grown in containers. However, Japanese Irises are more sensitive than any other irises to the acid/alkali balance of the soil. Acid soil (pH 5.5 to 6.5) is a definite requirement; lime in any form seems to be quickly fatal to these plants. It is not known whether it is alkalinity *per se* or the presence of calcium that causes their demise.

Based on their growth cycle, the ideal time to plant new rhizomes or divide established clumps would appear to be just after blooming, but growers in more southerly regions favor September for this chore, choosing to avoid the weeks of heat that follow the blooming season. Farther north (in northern, inland New England, Pennsylvania, and New York, as well as the upper Midwest), spring planting might be more successful. Spring planting, however, generally sacrifices that year's bloom.

WATER CULTURE

Japanese irises can be planted in as much as 8 in. of water, though this depth is not ideal. It seems that the presence of no more than 3 in. to 4 in. of water over the rhizomes during the spring and summer will give the best results.

Equally successful is the practice of siting the plants beside water, where the roots can easily reach saturated soil. The typical garden pool or larger pond is loaded with nutrients from decaying algae, aquatic vegetation, and fish, so soil amendment is not really neccessary; only in the smallest pools will fertilizer have to be added. Pellets used to feed other pool plants will work well with Japanese Irises.

The rhizomes should be set with the roots well spread out, and the junction between the leaf fan and the rhizome should be 2 in. to 3 in. below the surface of the soil (because of their upright style of growth, Japanese Iris rhizomes need to be planted more deeply than rhizomes of other irises). Newly arrived or purchased rhizomes should be kept in buckets of water during the planting process, and under no conditions should the roots become dry.

Experience indicates that water over the rhizomes in the winter can be harmful or even fatal, especially if it freezes. The best solution is to draw down the level of the pond so that the iris clumps are barely exposed, then mulch them heavily. In spring, when the water level is restored, the mulch will slowly decay and contribute nutrients.

Japanese Irises grown in ponds require division and resetting much less often than border plantings, generally only about every four or five years, provided the vertically growing rhizomes do not get too far above the soil level. This is a special danger if the pond is drawn down during the winter, since exposed rhizomes will be damaged by freezing and thawing.

CULTURE IN GARDEN BEDS

Despite the attractions of water culture and the extraordinary effects achieved in Japanese public gardens by masses of blooming irises in canals and ponds, most North American enthusiasts grow their Japanese Irises in ordinary garden beds, where the plants thrive with some extra watering.

Good soil preparation and attention to proper planting are extremely important. A heavy clay soil, acidic and with abundant organic matter, is ideal. The soil should be tilled to a depth of at least 1 ft.; Japanese Iris roots penetrate deeply. Large amounts of compost, rotted leaves, bark, sawdust or wood chips, well-composted animal manure, and even peat moss make good soil amendments. Remember that feeding the soil with organic matter feeds the microorganisms that will in turn provide much of the nutrition for your plants.

Japanese Irises are greedy feeders, and many authorities recommend adding some commercial fertilizer to the soil. Rather than that, I would suggest supplementing the organic matter with blood or cottonseed meal, or with superphosphate; I've noticed particularly wonderful results with the latter. Follow the package directions for any of these products. If you do use a commercial, packaged fertilizer, get one that is balanced for acid-loving plants such as azaleas, camellias, and hollies.

Planting the rhizomes
With Japanese Irises, the key to successful planting is never to let the roots of the plants dry out. New plants supplied by reputable growers will usually have from three to five rhizomes and leaf fans; keep the rhizomes in

buckets or pans of water until they can be planted. Newly arrived mail-order plants should be soaked in water for several days until new, white branch roots appear.

Dig a planting hole at least 10 in. deep and 18 in. wide and spread out the iris roots (not rhizomes!) over the sides of a small mound you have built in the center. Refill the hole so that the junction between leaf fan and rhizome is at least 3 in. below the surface, and so that the new plant is in the center of a bowl-shaped depression (photo, below right). Water thoroughly, filling the bowl two or three times, and repeat the watering every few days for two weeks, until the new plants are established and begin to put out new leaves.

Spacing is determined by how long you plan to leave your plants in place; placing them on 2-ft. centers will give you three to four years. Japanese Irises are not particularly good competitors with other fibrous-rooted perennials, so space them well away from companions such as daylilies. Lilies and daffodils, which complement the irises nicely, root at a deeper level and will not compete so much with them.

Care after planting
Mulch is good for Japanese Irises. When the plants have begun to establish themselves, fill the depression around them with coarse compost, leaf mold (photo, p. 112) or perhaps more durable materials such as ground bark. Avoid peat moss; it can form an impenetrable crust when dry and is difficult to wet again. Peat moss also absorbs a great deal of water and can prevent rain or irrigation from reaching the soil. The ideal mulch lets water through freely but prevents evaporation from the surface.

Through the life of the planting, renew the mulch layer each spring by adding new organic material. As it decays, it will feed the soil and thus the plants. Supplementing with commercial fertilizer is recommended by many growers (see p. 111), but my own Japanese Irises do very well with just a 2-in. layer of leaf mold added each spring.

Fall cleanup is important in order to limit damage from foliage thrips (see pp. 114-115) but foliage should not be removed until it is brown and withered. I have found that the removal of green leaves prematurely has an inhibiting effect on the next year's bloom.

Plant the rhizomes of Japanese Irises in a bowl-shaped depression in the garden, and flood the plants several times with water.

Leaf mold makes a good mulch for newly established Japanese Irises.

Japanese Irises multiply rapidly, and because the rhizomes do not spread out, plantings can become crowded. In addition, the vertical growth of the rhizomes brings them closer and closer to and even above the surface of the soil. Roots are produced only from the upper, active parts of the rhizome, so those at or near the surface are poorly anchored and cannot obtain enough water. After about three years in one place, the clumps should be divided and replanted, following the basic planting instructions described above. Take the opportunity to dig more compost into the soil!

CULTURE IN CONTAINERS

For centuries, Japanese gardeners have grown their irises in pots. Space is at a premium in Japan, and pot culture allows them to enjoy these plants in a restricted space and also to bring the fresh blooms indoors for close-up appreciation. Japanese aesthetes may spend many pleasant hours watching the blooms of

the potted irises slowly unfold in the serene surroundings of the traditionally spare Japanese room. For Americans and Europeans, container culture serves some of the same purposes. It is also a way to restore health to ailing garden plants.

Generally no more than one or two rhizomes of blooming size are set in a pot, and the pot should be the equivalent of a gallon nursery container. The choice of pots is wide. Traditional clay pots can be used, as well as plastic ones. The advantage of plastic is its greater moisture-retaining capability. If clay pots are used, those with a glaze on the outside are best.

Plants should be trimmed back to about 6 in. of leaves and roots and potted in a rich organic mixture. I've been successful using nothing but compost or leaf mold. In Japan, boiled sawdust is a favorite medium, though I suspect that nearly all nutrients would have to be supplied artificially. Even with richer soil mixtures, because of the small volume of the pot, feeding with a soluble commercial plant food is necessary. Use the kind specially formulated for acid-loving plants, such as orchids or azaleas.

The potted plants should spend the late summer and fall standing in 2 in. to 3 in. of water. A child's wading pool could hold a score of pots, or just two or three can be maintained in plastic washtubs. Site the tubs or pools in full sun, if possible, and replenish the water as needed.

If the plants are to winter outside (and this is recommended), take them out of the water, stand them on the ground, and cover them with a heavy layer of light material, such as pine needles or straw, to protect them against the freeze/thaw cycle. When Japanese Irises planted in the garden have begun to grow, the potted plants can be uncovered and restored to their place in the pool or washtub. They should bloom a little earlier than those planted in the ground, and once in bloom, they can be moved to a place where they can be fully enjoyed.

Annual repotting is a requirement for plants grown this way. Divide the clumps into one or two rhizomes each and replant in entirely fresh planting mix.

If by some chance you have not divided clumps of Japanese Iris growing in the garden in a timely fashion and the rhizomes have emerged above the soil with so few roots that they are in decline, container culture can save your plants. Treat them as described above, and when they recover their health, replant them in the garden.

Diseases and Pests

Especially when grown in water, Japanese Irises are rarely attacked by diseases and pests. In particular, they seem not to be affected by fungal and bacterial afflictions of the leaves and rhizomes. Problems may occasionally be caused by nematodes or iris borers, but the major danger comes from thrips.

NEMATODES

In some areas, notably California and the southern Midwest, nematodes sometimes attack Japanese Irises. These microscopic worms burrow in the roots of the plants and cause tumor-like growths. General decline in health and the presence of these root nodules are signs of nematode infestation.

The harmful nematodes cannot survive in saturated soil, so water culture or frequent flooding takes care of them. There is also some indication that nematodes are less of a problem in heavier, more organically rich soils, perhaps because these soils support populations of nematode predators, including a curious fungus that traps the nematodes in doughnut-shaped snares. If nematode infestations become heavy, only extreme measures, such as soil fumigation, are effective (see p. 54).

IRIS BORERS

Iris borers are seldom a problem with Japanese Irises—they much prefer the bearded types. If the occasional borer appears in a Japanese Iris planting, it can be dealt with by mechanical means. Borer caterpillars emerge in spring and begin to nibble the edges of iris leaves. They soon find their way into the center of the leaf fan, where they may cut off the younger, more delicate leaves entirely. At this point, you can seize the fan between your thumb and fingers and squeeze it, killing the caterpillar.

In the very unlikely event of a large-scale infestation, the remedy is spraying with a systemic insecticide that contains the compound dimethoate. Treat the planting when the leaf fans are about 6 in. tall, and again about two weeks later. For a detailed discussion of this pest, see pp. 54-57.

Thrips

The only serious insect pests of Japanese Irises are a few sorts of thrips. Thrips (the word is both singular and plural) are tiny, elongated insects that punch or scrape holes in the cells of leaves and flowers and suck out the contents. When they do this to actively growing or expanding parts of the plant, the new growth will be distorted and twisted. Thrips breed with unbelievable rapidity and can do a great deal of damage in a short time.

The iris foliage thrips is a covert feeder, spending its time inside the folded leaves. Damage is signaled by distorted new growth, often with reddish streaks; heavily attacked plants decline quickly. Flower thrips cause only minor damage to a planting unless they are present in great numbers, in which case you will be sickened by the sight of flowers crawling with hundreds of tiny insects (photo, below left).

Systemic insecticides are effective controls on thrips, and work best if they are applied before the thrips appear. If you noticed a problem in the spring, you should probably apply a treatment the following spring. Since the thrips eggs overwinter on old foliage, a good fall cleanup is helpful in preventing infestations.

More Irises for Wet Spots

The species and varieties mentioned below are not so readily available as Japanese Irises, but for the most part thrive on the same cultural conditions. *Iris laevigata,* however, requires more water, and *I. versicolor* and its hybrids more easily adapt to ordinary border conditions.

It seems to me that the species listed here, all quite interfertile, make up a complex that could in the future rival the Japanese and Louisiana Irises in popularity because of their wonderful range of variation and their wide adaptability. Watch for them!

Iris pseudacorus

Many years ago, when still a student, I fancied that I had discovered a new species of iris growing in a boggy spot on our old family homestead, where nothing of man seemed to have remained except a slowly collapsing cellar

This bloom of 'Frills and Spangles' is heavily infested with thrips (small white flecks). They do little harm to the flower itself but are not pleasant to see.

Iris pseudacorus, native to Europe, has escaped from gardens and naturalized over much of the United States and Canada.

hole. But an understanding botanist explained, somehow without dampening my enthusiasm, that what I had found was a well-known European species, *Iris pseudacorus*. This clump had probably been planted 50 years before by my grandparents, who were both keen gardeners. This species (photo, above) is a native of Europe. It often escapes from gardens and is now established in much of the northeastern United States.

Iris pseudacorus is one of the largest of all irises when it comes to the bulk of the plant; when growing in rich swampy soil, its stiff, robust leaves can be more than 6 ft. tall! On the other hand, plants of the same clone grown in an ordinary herbaceous border may be only about 2 ft. tall.

The rhizomes are very large, perhaps the biggest of all iris, and give rise to many branches, each with a fan of thick, deep green leaves. (According to iris authority Brian Mathew, the powdered rhizomes were used by medieval herbalists as a powerful laxative. I haven't tried it.)

Blooming at about the middle of the Tall Bearded Iris season, *Iris pseudacorus* produces an abundance of branched 3-ft. stalks bearing bright yellow flowers about 3 in. in diameter. Each fall petal is typically marked with a circlet of purple dashes that appear brown against the yellow of the petal.

As with any plant that has been in cultivation for a long time, many varieties have been selected. Pale cream ('Primrose Monarch') and nearly white ('Alba') flowers are found in many of these, and others are even deeper yellow,

The variety of *Iris pseudacorus* with variegated foliage has tremendous garden value. The yellow-striped foliage will turn all green later in the summer.

'Holden Clough' is an *Iris pseudacorus* hybrid with yellow flowers veined in brownish purple. The other parent is unknown but may be *Iris foetidissima.*

without the brown markings on the falls ('Golden Queen'). A true double is also found, but looks unfortunately like a wad of yellowish tissue paper. Perhaps most interesting is the variety 'Variegata', in which the flowers are as usual, but the young spring foliage is strikingly marked with cream (photo, above left). Too bad that this effect fades in the summer and the leaves turn all green.

Breeders have been hard at work with this species, which seems to cross freely with many other irises. It has been used to bring yellow into the spectrum of the Japanese Irises. A clever bee effected a cross between *I. pseudacorus* and *I. foetidissma* (see pp. 138-139) that was introduced as 'Holden Clough' (the second word is pronounced "cluff"), with yellow

pseudacorus-like flowers entirely veined over in brownish purple, giving a bright brown effect at a distance (photo, above right).

Iris pseudacorus is easily grown from either purchased rhizomes or its abundantly produced seed. Of course, if one of the named varieties is what you desire, you'll have to buy rhizomes. Seeds can produce a wide range of types. The seeds can be sown directly in the garden in the fall, to germinate the following spring (see pp. 148-152 for tips on growing irises from seeds; those directions will work for *I. pseudacorus).*

Iris pseudacorus, though at its best near or in water, will also bloom well under garden condtions. This most adaptable iris seems not very particular about soil so long as it does not dry out. However, it is a truly spectacular and trouble-free plant for rich organic soil near the pond or stream margin and can stand submergence year round. It appears to be entirely hardy at least to USDA Zone 4.

IRIS LAEVIGATA

In Japan, the popularity of *Iris laevigata* is not nearly so great as that of the *I. ensata*-derived Japanese Irises, but this distinctive Asian native has been in cultivation for at least as long, and varieties mentioned in Japanese gardening books in the late 1600s are still in existence. The Japanese name for the species is Kakitsubata.

Iris laevigata differs from the Japanese Irises in being more dependent on water (photo, right) and in lacking the strong midrib of the foliage. The flowers, too, have not been so strongly changed from the wild form and are typically iris-like, with erect standards. Shades of blue, purple, and violet predominate, with some unique color patterns, including types that appear as white flowers lightly spattered with blue ink ('Washino-o'), and dark purples strikingly bordered with white ('Maikujaku').

A further intriguing feature is that some varieties are nearly ever-blooming in mild climates. I recall seeing a large clump in the pool at the Berkeley, California, Botanical Garden that bore both mature seed pods and freshly opening flowers in October. This trait would be worth passing on to other irises, and indeed *Iris laevigata* can be crossed with nearly all of the other irises mentioned in this chapter. However, developments now seem to focus on hybrids with the American *I. versicolor,* called Versi-Laevs.

While some success has been reported growing *Iris laevigata* under ordinary garden conditions, most reports say that a marshy spot or actual standing water is required. Perhaps this lesser degree of adaptability has limited the popularity of this otherwise lovely and graceful iris. In any case, named varieties, or any forms at all, are difficult to find in the United States. This situation should change as water gardening becomes more popular; for sources try pond-plant specialists.

Iris laevigata, a Japanese native, is a true water iris ideal for the garden pool. This is the form of the species with foliage variegated in white.

IRIS VIRGINICA AND IRIS VERSICOLOR

Iris virginica, the Great Blue Flag of the southeastern United States, is a giant that rivals *I. pseudacorus.* Well-grown plants at the water's edge can top 6 ft., but the flower stems are only about 3 ft. tall, with 3-in. or 4-in. flowers. Color variants include a pretty white, reddish violets, and veined forms, in addition to the more usual blue-violet (photo, below left). Unlike *I. laevagata, I. virginica* can adapt to garden conditions away from bogs or standing water, but as a much smaller plant than when grown there.

In an interesting botanical detective story, Edgar Anderson demonstrated 60 years ago that *Iris versicolor,* the other common iris species of the eastern United States (photo, below right), was the offspring of *I. virginica* and another species, *I. setosa* (see the sidebar on pp. 108-109). Evidently these two species, which do not now grow together, co-occurred when the advance of the ancient glaciers forced the more northerly *I. setosa* southward. The new hybrid species, *versicolor,* inherited a full set of chromosomes from both its parents, and so has a total of 108, the most of any iris species, and nearly a record for any plant.

Iris virginica (above) succeeds in southern and northern gardens alike. Selections are available in a range of colors. This light-blue seedling was raised by the author.

Iris versicolor in a typical natural setting (right), a roadside wetland in northern Pennsylvania.

'Mysterious Monique' shows the great range of color and pattern that is typical of *Iris versicolor*.

'Gerald Darby' is a hybrid of *Iris virginica* and *Iris versicolor*. It is seen here with a pure white selection of *I. virginica*.

In keeping with its genetic potential—and its name—*I. versicolor* is vigorous and highly variable, with flowers ranging from pure white through blue-violets to reddish purple in a wide range of patterns. My personal favorite is 'Candy Striper', which is white with bright reddish veins. 'Mysterious Monique,' a dramatic variety with deep violet falls (photo, above left), is rapidly growing in popularity. *Iris versicolor* has a more northerly range than *I. virginica* and is probably hardy well into USDA Zone 3. It is a prominent feature of the Maine coast and of the Canadian Maritimes as well, and is found around the Great Lakes.

Iris versicolor is not nearly so dependent on water in the garden as *I. laevigata* and does well in a border, despite always being found around water in the wild. Given its tremendous genetic potential, it seems strange that this species

has not had more attention from breeders. However, at least one commercial firm in Canada has an intensive program going, led by Tony Huber, and a few United States specialists, such as Marty Schafer and Jan Sacks, are emerging.

Iris versicolor crosses easily with Japanese irises (Versatas), *I. laevigata,* and, of course, *I. virginica.* The hybrids with *virginica* are called *Iris × robusta,* and include the worthwhile 'Gerald Darby', a medium-blue plant of extraordinary vigor and with striking deep wine-colored stems and leaf bases (photo, above right). A few hybrids between *I. versicolor* and Siberian Irises have also been reported.

IRISES FOR DRIER SPOTS

The irises described in this chapter are a diverse bunch, drawn from both the bearded and beardless groups. They are united, however, in that they are capable of thriving under periodically quite dry conditions. Some of them, such as the Spuria Irises, hail from climates where warm, dry summers give way to wetter, cooler conditions in winter and spring. Others, such as the Aril Irises, are native to harsh deserts. Still others, such as some of the Arilbred hybrids, may need abundant water during their period of growth, but prefer to dry out when they go dormant.

Spuria Irises

In older gardens, some of them long abandoned, you may find a broad clump of an extraordinarily vigorous iris, with tall, tough, unblemished, strap-like leaves. The large flowers, held on stalks more than 4 ft. tall, are likely to be either brilliant yellow, or white with a wide yellow patch on the falls. The yellow-flowered plants will very likely prove to be the species *Iris crocea,* and the white ones, *I. orientalis.* The stalks are spire-like, with the branches being held close to the stem, looking more a gladiolus spike than the stem of a flowering iris.

These statuesque plants are representatives of the Spuria Irises, whose long lives and qualities of persistence make them some of the last plants to disappear (if they ever do) from old gardens. One of the great selling points of these irises is that they will carry on as ever-expanding clumps for a decade or more without having to be dug up, divided, and reset. The other side of this coin, of course, is that they tend to resent disturbance and may take time to bloom from newly planted rhizomes.

Because of their vigor and ability to compete with other plants and because they need not be dug and divided often, Spurias are perhaps better suited to the mixed border than any other irises, even the Siberians. While the most commonly grown forms are tall (a few hybrids can top 5 ft.), there are also dwarf species, such as *Iris graminea* (see the sidebar on p. 125).

The tall hybrids should be placed near the back of the border, and the dwarfs make a delightful edging. Good companions for Spurias are lilies (photo, above right), which bloom somewhat later, as well as chrysanthemums and hemerocallis, extending the bloom season well into autumn. Earlier flowers can be provided by spring-flowering bulbs, whose ripening foliage will be hidden by that of the other plants. Low-growing annuals also mix well into a planting that features Spuria Irises.

Spuria Irises harmonize well with other border stars, such as Asiatic hybrid lilies. 'Sonoran Skies' is shown here.

The wild species of the Series Spuriae are found growing from western Europe, through the Middle East, Turkey, and Russia (their real stronghold), and into the mountains of western China. The two tall species already mentioned have been widely distributed by man as well, and are naturalized in many parts of the world.

Compared to the breeding of Tall Bearded Irises and Siberians, hybridizers have paid relatively little attention to Spuria Irises. Sir Michael Foster, the great British iris pioneer, introduced a few hybrids in the 1880s and 1890s. Later, the main interest in the group shifted to the United States, the western part of which offers almost ideal conditions for their cultivation.

THE PLANTS

The tough Spuria foliage springs from an elongate, hard rhizome that habitually grows 2 in. or more beneath the surface of the ground and is anchored by long, thong-like roots. The growth of the rhizome is different from that of most irises. After leaves appear above ground in the spring, the rhizome significantly elongates, but the older leaves remain fresh and green and attached to it. As a result, the fan opens up and becomes elongated in the direction of the rhizome's growth.

A few months after the blooming season (which follows on the heels of the Tall Bearded season), the foliage may disappear entirely. By this time the growing tip of the rhizome has extended a few inches beyond the leaf fan, forming a compact underground bud that will be the source of new leaves when rains return. Also unlike most irises, old rhizomes can bloom again as the growing point extends beyond the bloomstalk.

THE FLOWERS

Spuria Iris flowers have an elegant appearance and are as varied in form as those of the Siberians, but in general they are reminiscent of the bulbous Dutch irises, favorites of florists. Varieties closest to the species have narrow, arching petals. The falls of these forms have a

'Purple Concerto' (above) has the broad falls and light ruffling popular in modern Spuria Irises.

Glowing chestnut brown highlighted with yellow (right) is a color combination unique to Spuria Irises.

long basal portion (the haft) which expands broadly into an almost circular blade at the tip, while the narrow standards are carried erect. Large style arms, important contributors in this case to the appearance of the blooms, arch out over the falls.

By means of selection, more recent hybridizers have produced blooms with shorter hafts and broader, ruffled blades in the falls, as well as wider standards that are often spreading (photo at left, facing page). Like peony buds, all Spurias produce copious supplies of nectar from the bases of the petals, which attracts ants.

The color range is wide, embracing whites, with or without large yellow patches on the falls, to oranges and vibrant coppery or chestnut browns (photo at right, facing page), some approaching black from this unusual side. Purples, lavenders, and blues are prominent, sometimes combined with yellow or copper in an extraordinarily striking way. Even pinkish shades have begun to appear.

Growing Spuria Irises

Spuria Irises are not often available from general nurseries, though some can supply *I. orientalis*. Specialist nurseries in Spurias are concentrated in the western part of the country, particularly California, and several are listed on pp. 162-165. Like most beardless irises, they are shipped packed in plastic bags, so that the roots can be kept moist.

Spuria Irises are easily grown, delightful garden subjects that can be extraordinarily long-lived in borders or in dedicated plantings. But there are some things about them that you need to understand if your Spuria plantings are to be successful.

GENERAL CULTURAL REQUIREMENTS

Spuria Irises in their native haunts occupy a very wide range of habitats, if the group is taken as a whole. Some are found in meadow settings, with moisture available much of the year, and the most common European species actually favor wet habitats. One European native is called *Iris halophila* ("salt-loving"), since it has a marked tolerance for salt and can grow in saline marshes. Others are plants of strongly seasonal climates, with a well-defined dry season in late summer (these species are the parents of most of the commercially available American hybrids). Still others are found high in the mountains, growing among rocks and scrub.

Given this wide range of habitats, it is difficult to draw any firm conclusions about growing Spurias from such information. In fact, reading about Spurias can produce a real feeling of schizophrenia—the British books recommend them for sites moister than those that support Tall Bearded Irises, while the American books tout their drought-resistant qualities. Let's rely on the experience of a couple of generations of American gardeners. This experience has shown that the prime areas for Spurias are in the western parts of the country, where summers are dry. But Spurias remain an option for the Midwest and East as well, if the right conditions can be provided, and hybridizers are continuing to work on varieties that do well in the eastern part of the country. Most Spuria varieties are hardy into USDA Zone 5, or even farther north.

Soil and sun

Since most American-grown Spuria varieties come from progenitors that like a dry summer dormant period, excellent drainage is vital. However, light, sandy soils do not grow good Spurias. Instead, a heavier clay-based soil, rich in organic matter, is required. Spurias are greedy feeders, and a layer of compost or manure shoveled over the clumps before growth begins in the fall will be of great benefit.

Some growers also use packaged fertilizers, and an ordinary lawn fertilizer (10-10-10) seems to work quite well when given in the spring and again in early fall, but don't overdo it. Too much fertilizer will encourage lush, soft growth that can easily be taken off by rot in a wet summer. If adequate nitrogen is already available, use

rock phosphate as a top dressing instead of a balanced fertilizer. The acidity or alkalinity of the soil does not appear to be of very great importance, so long as extremes are avoided.

In most gardens in the Northeast and Midwest, Spurias will require full sun, but in the more southerly areas and the desert Southwest, some afternoon shade will be appreciated.

PLANTING THE RHIZOMES

The fact that Spuria Irises have two periods of growth, spring and fall, suggests that either early-spring or late-summer planting will succeed. However, in my Zone 7a garden, I prefer to plant in the late summer, when the mild weather of the coming autumn will provide good conditions for establishment.

Prepare your Spuria planting site by digging the soil deeply and incorporating plenty of organic material, especially compost or aged cow manure or horse manure. These amendments will support big populations of soil microbes whose activities will provide much of the nutrition required. Since Spurias slowly form large clumps that can remain in place even for decades, space the rhizomes well apart, perhaps as much as on 3-ft. centers.

Newly purchased rhizomes should never be allowed to dry out completely, as this will cause them to lose their roots, a setback that may delay bloom for two years or more. The planting holes need to be at least 1 ft. deep so that the roots can be well spread out and the rhizomes set horizontally a few inches beneath the surface. Cover them and water well. No further watering should be needed.

Delicacy and refinement characterize the Spuria Iris.

IRIS GRAMINEA

Iris graminea is a diminutive member of the Series Spuriae, rarely exceeding 8 in. in height. It can be found in the wild in southern Europe and Russia. The flowers, about 3 in. in diameter, are of typical Spuria Iris form. Up to three or four of them are carried on each bloomstalk.

The standards are a rosy violet shade, while the falls have a large white area veined with violet, coming together into a violet patch at the tip of the blade (photo, right). The large style arms of pale rose pink, with just a hint of lavender, contribute a great deal to the flower's attractiveness. With many, but not all, of the plants in this species, there is often a delightful fragrance present, which has led to the common name of Plum-Scented Iris.

As the name of the species suggests, the foliage of *I. graminea* is tough and grasslike. At blooming time, it just barely exceeds the height of the

Iris graminea, a dwarf Spuria Iris, holds its attractive blooms down in the foliage.

flowering stems, then elongates to a height of up to 2 ft. before withering away for the summer. Late in the fall, with rain and cool weather, the leaves reappear.

This little Spuria is able to grow and bloom in partial shade, a rare feature for an iris. I've got it growing at the front of a border and among boulders in a rock garden; both of these areas are shaded during the afternoon. The plants seems to like being snuggled in between boulders and will quickly fill the available space.

Iris graminea is rarely available as plants, though it seems not to mind being transplanted as much as the larger Spuria Irises. Luckily for the iris enthusiast, it is easily grown from seed, and seedlings bloom within two to three years. Increase thereafter is rapid, and a substantial clump results.

CARING FOR THE PLANTS

Within a few weeks, late-summer-planted Spurias will show new leaf growth above the surface, which may reach a height of 1 ft. to 2 ft. before slowing down and stopping for the winter. For newly set plants, a winter mulch may be advisable, mainly to extend the time available for root growth and to protect the fresh foliage. In the mild climates of southern California and Arizona, winter mulch is not necessary.

With the approach of spring, growth will resume and soon the tall, impressive spikes of bloom will rise above the leaves. After blooming,

Spurias may grow on for a time before starting to go dormant for the summer. At this time old leaves and stalks should be removed and disposed of, and the foliage may be cut down completely once it shows signs of departing.

Summer moisture is a problem for some Spurias because it can encourage the growth of fungi and bacteria that destroy the buried rhizomes. Some of the older hybrids, particularly those that bloom in blue or purple shades, may be especially susceptible to crown rot (see pp. 126-127), but with good drainage most of the more modern varieties seem much less inclined to disappear in wet summers.

'Royal Cadet', a pastel Spuria Iris.

Strong contrast in colors is seen in Spuria Iris.

Just as growth begins in the fall, top-dress the Spurias with a layer of compost or well-rotted manure to refresh the organic content of the soil. This is a procedure that greatly encourages these plants.

Division of old clumps becomes necessary only after many years have passed. It is best carried out in the fall.

Diseases and Pests of Spuria Irises

Like most irises, Spurias are remarkably healthy plants. They are only occasionally bothered by diseases such as iris mosaic virus and crown rot. And aside from aphids, the usual insect pests, such as the iris borer, do not seem to be very interested in Spuria Irises.

IRIS MOSAIC VIRUS

Iris mosaic virus can disfigure Spuria Irises, distorting and flecking the foliage and causing stripes to appear in the flowers. There is no cure, but newer varieties show a high degree of resistance.

CROWN ROT

Mustard-seed fungus, described in detail on pp. 50-51, causes problems in wet summers, after the plants have bloomed. The bases of leaves show a webbing of fungi, accompanied later by tiny brown or black spherical bodies called sclerotia (the "mustard seeds" from which the fungus gets its name). The growing points of the rhizomes can be destroyed. To control this disease, spray with a systemic fungicide (consult a local cooperative extension agent for a recommendation) just as the bloomstalks appear, and repeat at least twice until the plants go dormant. It has also been recommended that newly acquired rhizomes be soaked for a few hours before planting in a 5% solution of bleach (sodium hypochlorite).

Aphids

Viruses are transmitted from plant to plant by aphids (greenflies). These find plenty of places to hide in the leafy bloomstalks of Spuria Irises, and as the nectar produced by the flowers draws ants, the ants may bring along their domesticated aphids (several ant species keep aphid "cattle," which they milk for a sugary secretion). Prompt removal of spent bloomstalks will control aphid infestations; alternatively, treatments with insecticidal soap or a systemic insecticide containing dimethoate will also work.

Aril Irises

In 1926, the great American painter Georgia O'Keeffe produced one of her most famous works, *Black Iris III.* Living in New York City at the time, O'Keeffe haunted the flower markets and took home blooms to paint that appealed to her. She searched every spring for her favorite, the black iris, sometimes finding it, sometimes not. The student of irises will quickly recognize the black iris as an Oncocyclus Iris, a member of the Aril group.

The Arils are a group of bearded irises that get their name from their peculiar seeds, each of which bears at one end a white knob called an aril. Although it has not been demonstrated for these irises, arils in other plants are often rich food packets that are designed for a particular purpose. They attract ants or other insects, which carry off the seed, eat the aril, and then drop the seed some distance from the parent plant. This curious method of distribution ensures that a plant's own offspring will not become its immediate competitors, and by keeping them some distance away, may also help to avoid inbreeding. In nature, Aril Irises are found in deserts and dry mountain meadows, where this distributional feature would aid in survival.

There are five groups of Aril Irises: the Oncocycli (or Oncos, for short), Regelias (or Hexapogons), Pseudoregelias, Psammirises, and Falcifolias. The latter three are small collections of dwarf species that are very rarely grown, though some Psammirises have contributed genes to modern Dwarf Bearded hybrids. We'll focus here on Oncos and Regelias, and their hybrids with each other (Regeliocycli) and with various other bearded irises (Arilbreds).

Oncocycli

With more than 50 species named (though some are probably just variants of others), form and color are extremely varied among the Oncos, including wine reds and bright yellows as well as the more typical violets and purples. Exotic patterns are the keynote, often expressed as bold veining or as dots ranging from fine pinpricks to large spots of color. Most species have a huge signal patch of black or violet on each fall petal, probably serving as a guide to pollinating insects. The flowers may be very large or quite small, and the height of the plant ranges from a few inches to a couple of feet.

The largest of the Oncos, and one of the most spectacular of all irises, is *Iris gatesii*, often referred to as the Prince of Irises. Like most Oncos, this species grows from small, hard, knobby, red rhizomes with a curiously pleasing fragrance. Its foliage is surprisingly sparse for the size of the flower that is to come, and each gray-green leaf is curved outward like a sickle. The 1-ft. to 2-ft. bloomstalk bears only a single terminal flower, but what a flower! Broadly globular in form, it may be over 7 in. in diameter. From a distance it gives the impression of being gray, but close inspection reveals a creamy white ground that is very finely veined and dotted with violet. The beard is broad and diffuse, a patch of scattered blackish hairs, and the broad style arms are strongly thrust out over the falls.

Iris susiana is another stunning member of this clan (photo at left, facing page). Its flower is similar in size to *I. gatesii* (though rarely so tall), with the veining and dotting a very dark purple on a whiter background, and the beard sits on a large spot of nearly jet black. In cultivation for centuries, it has been long known as the Mourning Iris for its somber coloration.

In nature there appear to be two groups of Oncos. One, which is found in the mountain ranges of Turkey, Iran, and the Caucasus, has very hardy species, while the other, which is found in the deserts of the Middle East and Asia Minor, is less hardy. Both groups, however, are true xerophytes, or dry-ground plants, and are quite intolerant of moisture except when they are in active growth. Leaf production may begin in early winter, and soon after the spring bloom season (typically about tulip time), the leaves wither away and the plants go completely dormant. During this time, they must be protected from moisture, and many forms need a good, hot baking in utterly dry soil.

REGELIAS

The Regelia Irises are in strong contrast to the Oncos, despite their close relationship. Where Onco flowers are generously globular, Regelia flowers tend to have narrow, tailored petals, the standards held rigidly upright, the falls nearly perfectly vertical. Exemplary of this flower form is the species *Iris korolkowii.* (photo at right, facing page). As with other Regelias, this species has two buds per unbranched stem. The typical form has a white or pale-violet ground with stark, broad veins of purple or brown radiating from the petal bases. Not only the falls, but also the standards are bearded; another name for the half-dozen species of the Regelia section is Hexapogon ("six-bearded").

Two other species in this group that are much in demand among collectors are *Iris stolonifera* (see the photo at right on p. 15) and *I. hoogiana*. *Iris stolonifera* is an attractive species with a number of named varieties, but usually with petals of blue or lavender edged and veined in bright brown, set off by an electric blue beard on the falls. As the name says, the rhizomes send out long stolons, or underground runners, at the ends of which new rhizomes develop. Like *I. stolonifera, I. hoogiana* is a tetraploid, with four sets of chromosomes as opposed to the usual two. Its lovely, tailored, if somewhat narrow blooms are an extraordinary blue, with a wonderful silky reflection.

Since the Regelias are plants of mountain meadows from Iran to central Asia, they are less sensitive to moisture during their dormancy, and therefore a bit easier to grow than the Oncos. In fact, they need abundant moisture in early spring to simulate the melting of the heavy snow that covers them in winter. All the Regelias are quite hardy, probably at least to USDA Zone 4.

Iris susiana (far left), with its globular form and somber veining in deep violet, epitomizes the Oncocyclus Irises.

Iris korolkowii (left), a Regelia Iris, has narrow, tailored petals of cream, widely veined in dark brown or purple.

REGELIOCYCLI, ONCOBREDS, AND ARILBREDS

Late in the 19th century, the Dutch bulb growers of the Van Tubergen family crossed a number of Onco species with the Regelia *I. korolkowii,* producing a line of hybrids called Regeliocycli. Most of the new varieties, introduced from 1895 on, were given names from Greek and Roman mythology, such as 'Theseus' and 'Venus'. These hybrids (photo at left, p. 130) were neatly intermediate between their parents, most inheriting strong veined patterns from *I. korolkowii.* They have hybrid vigor, and when they can be obtained they are as easily grown as the Regelias.

From this beginning, a bewildering array of hybrids involving Oncos, Regelias and Tall Bearded Irises has gradually evolved. For example, the Van Tubergen family produced 'Ib-Mac', by crossing the Onco *I. iberica* with 'Macrantha', a Tall Bearded Iris. In the United States, 'William Mohr', from crossing *I. gatesii*

with 'Parisiana' (a diploid Tall Bearded hybrid), appeared in 1925. 'Ib-Mac' and 'William Mohr' were crossed in the late 1930s to give 'Capitola', which has very fertile pollen.

From 'Capitola' crossed to Tall Bearded varieties of all sorts came an array of so-called Oncobreds, with Onco-like flowers on Tall-Bearded-style plants. From their heritage, these are also called Mohrs, and one of them, 'Elmohr' won the Dykes Medal, the highest possible award from the American Iris Society. Since then, other highly fertile Oncobreds such as 'Esther the Queen' and 'Pro News' have largely replaced 'Capitola' and 'Ib-Mac' in breeding efforts. Today, hybrids of Arils with Tall Bearded Irises are so mixed in their heritage that the general term Arilbred is more often applied (photos, p. 132).

From the beginning, the goal of the hybridizer has been to put the exotic flowers of the purebred Aril Irises on plants that can be grown as easily as the Tall Bearded hybrids.

Admittedly, while progress has been made, there is a long way to go. Aril Iris enthusiasts have worked up a labyrinth of terminology for their hybrids, depending not only on the inclusion of Onco, Regelia and Tall Bearded genes, but on chromosome complement as well.

Growing Aril Irises

Irises in the Aril group are for the most part true desert plants, and as such are intolerant of summer moisture. Thus they are ideally adapted to the desert Southwest of the United States—and difficult to grow elsewhere. But if you properly prepare the soil and the site and invest time in plant care, you will be able to grow these exotic irises in many places that would otherwise be inhospitable to them. I've succeeded with them in climates as disparate as the mountains of northern Pennsylvania, humid central Virginia, and the New Mexico desert.

SITE AND SOIL

Although many of us associate deserts with sand, deserts are not always sandy. Many Onco species in their native habitats grow in heavy clay soils that bake to a rock-like texture in the

Regeliocyclus hybrids combine features of Oncocyclus and Regelia Irises. In the flower above, the influence of *Iris korolkowii* is clear.

'Aril Lady' (right) is an Arilbred hybrid.

summer. On the other hand, growers in moist climates have been successful using a light, sandy soil mix that drains quickly.

Two qualities of the soil aside from texture do appear to be important. First, the soil must be highly fertile. Arils have a very short period of growth, and the nutrients they need must be within reach of their extensive root systems. Desert soils are often proverbially rich in mineral nutrients, lacking only water to make them accessible to plants. Second, the soil must be alkaline and contain good amounts of calcium and magnesium. This requirement is best met by using slaked lime or ground limestone in quantity when preparing the bed, especially if the native soil is acid. Dolomitic limestone, which contains magnesium, is especially good.

If you are growing pure Aril Irises in dry-summer regions, a simple raised bed, with prepared fertile soil, may suffice. Experience indicates that organic matter, such as well-prepared compost, is beneficial. If the soil is not already alkaline with abundant calcium, slaked lime or ground limestone should be added. Authorities recommend up to 4 oz. of slaked lime per square meter of soil surface, and about twice as much ground limestone; the limestone has a slower, long-term effect. The bed should be prepared, amended, and watered thoroughly several times at least three weeks before planting.

If you are growing pure Aril Irises where summer rains are expected, the beds should be sited on a slope or in a place where drainage will be sharp. Old storm windows or plastic sheeting mounted on frames can be propped over the plants in summer to limit the amount of rain that reaches them. For really wet-summer areas, a bulb frame or similar structure (see the sidebar on p. 94) is strongly recommended.

TIMING THE PLANTING

Aril Iris rhizomes are usually shipped by speciality growers in late summer or fall. The rhizomes typically will be reddish, knobby, and sometimes with long runners extending from them. They will be entirely devoid of foliage and may even lack roots.

Nearly all purebred Arils begin growing immediately after they are planted and watered; for this reason it may be desirable to delay planting until late in the fall to avoid having soft foliage above ground, where it will be vulnerable to winter freezes. The Middle Eastern Oncos in particular are of uncertain hardiness and may benefit from winter protection with a light, airy mulch. The hardier Caucasus and Turkish Oncos, as well as the Regelias, can be planted earlier and usually will not need protection.

CARING FOR THE PLANTS

If the bed is in the open, natural rainfall and snowmelt will probably suffice through the winter. When the weather warms in spring, additional water will be required in desert gardens. Feeding with soluble fertilizer having a high potash and phosphate rating may be useful. Growth and bloom are swift, and since each flowering stem produces only one or two flowers, the season is short. Within a few weeks of blooming the foliage will begin to yellow and wither. At this point, any additional moisture is to be avoided. One strategy that can be used by gardeners in regions with summer rains is to dig the rhizomes, cure them thoroughly in the shade, and store them through the summer in a warm place.

Arilbreds such as 'Desert Finery' (far left) and the unnamed seedling at left are the result of crosses between Arils and Tall Bearded Irises. Both flowers have a large contrasting signal spot, passed on by its Oncocyclus ancestors.

This method worked well for me here in central Virginia: I packed the cured rhizomes in dry vermiculite in open paper bags and kept them in a shed that got quite warm on sunny summer days. But I must add that during a series of dry summers in the late 1980s, a number of purebred Arils survived and performed well here in the open ground without being dug up! Now, some 10 to 12 years later, a few plants still survive under the eaves of a building, against a south-facing brick wall. This seems to be a situation where experimentation is called for.

Before replanting in the fall, carefully separate the new rhizomes from the old ones, which can be discarded. Be sure that cuts or breaks dry thoroughly before you replant. Growers in some climates (usually those to which the plants are best adapted) report that heavy multiplication of rhizomes results in congested clumps in just one year. Under those conditions, it is probably wise to lift and divide the rhizomes every year.

GROWING ARILS IN CONTAINERS

Arils can be grown in containers. Plant single rhizomes of Aril Irises in 8-in.-dia., deep clay pots filled with a rich, but well-drained soil mix. Feed regularly with a soluble fertilizer, since the plants will quickly exhaust the limited nutrients available. After the plants flower, dry off the pots and store them in a warm place until repotting the following winter.

A WORD ABOUT ARILBREDS

Specific cultural recommendations for Arilbreds are difficult to make. How they are treated depends largely on the proportion of Aril and Tall Bearded genes; the more Aril "blood" present, the less tolerant they are likely to be of summer moisture. The Mohr type varieties, now more often called Quarterbreds, are about 75% Tall Bearded and can be grown under the same conditions, with a little more attention to good drainage. But hybrids that are mostly Aril may have to be treated much like the species.

Arilbreds may show a definite cessation of growth in the summer, but are not likely to lose their foliage completely. When they arrive from growers, Arilbred rhizomes usually still have their foliage and roots and should be planted in the same way as Tall Bearded Irises (see pp. 39-43). If the clumps get congested in just one season (this is most likely to happen in regions with dry summers), it's a good idea to lift and divide the rhizomes every year.

Diseases andPests of Arils and Arilbreds

As bearded irises, Arils and Arilbreds are subject to the same array of diseases and pests as Tall Bearded Irises (see pp. 49-57). Extraordinary vigilance against pests and diseases is required when growing these irises—their period of growth is so short that anything that weakens them during that time can eliminate the next year's blooms.

RHIZOME ROTS

Rhizome rots, both bacterial and fungal, are particularly dangerous to Arilbreds and can take a heavy toll. Avoiding excessive summer wetness seems to be the best approach, but if such maladies appear they can be treated as described on pp. 49-51.

LEAF SPOTS

Arils and Arilbreds are highly susceptible to the leaf-spot diseases that affect other bearded irises—the foliage can be destroyed and the plants seriously weakened. Fungal leaf spot can spread rapidly among Arilbreds; the foliage of pure Arils is usually gone so quickly that this pathogen doesn't get a chance to attack. Regular sprayings with a systemic fungicide will keep the leaves clean. All old foliage and flower stems should be removed and burned.

IRIS MOSAIC VIRUS

Iris mosaic virus is an intractable problem for Arils and Arilbreds, and most stocks are infected. The plants are weakened and the flowers may be irregularly streaked with purple or show "water spots." There is no cure. The only thing the gardener can do is to find resistant varieties or grow new plants from seed.

IRIS BORERS

Iris borers usually don't have time to attack the pure Aril Irises, but Arilbreds, with their more persistant foliage, are as likely as Tall Bearded Hybrids to suffer from this pest. Ways to deal with the problem are described on pp. 54-57.

APHIDS

Aphids (greenflies) suck sap from leaves and weaken the plants. They also transmit virus diseases from plant to plant. In small plantings, you can control aphids just by wiping them off leaves. For heavy infestations, use insecticidal soap, following the package directions.

IRISES FOR SPECIAL PLACES AND TIMES

Crested Irises for Light Shade

An Iris for Deep Shade

Pacific Coast Native Irises

Iris verna

An Iris that Blooms in Winter

Ready for some advanced irising? If you've successfully grown the Bearded Irises, Siberians or Spurias, Japanese Irises or Louisianas, you may be up for some of the more unusual specialties offered by the genus *Iris.* How about woodland irises that thrive in light and deep shade, or irises that bloom even earlier that the crocuses? This chapter will introduce you to all of these, and more.

Woodland garden environments are highly varied. They range from the partly sunny forest margins to the deep shade found under large trees. In between are all gradations of light intensity, and believe it or not, there are irises for each spot.

Crested Irises for Light Shade

In the dappled shade of open woods, wildflowers take advantage of the light that reaches the forest floor in early spring. Botanists

The Dwarf Crested Iris *(Iris cristata)*, a North American native, can form a blue carpet over the forest floor in early spring.

call these plants "ephemerals," because they flower and mature their foliage quickly, before the canopy of leaves closes in and blocks out the sun. Among the ephemerals are several Crested Iris species, two of them North American natives.

Crested Irises belong to the Section Lophiris. In these species, the fall petals bear a crest of finger-like projections, rather than a beard. However, they seem closely related to be the Bearded Irises, as testified to by the occasional hybrid between the two groups.

IRIS CRISTATA

Iris cristata, the Dwarf Crested Iris, can be found in woodlands throughout the Appalachian Mountains, from Pennsylvania to

Georgia and Alabama. It grows best in deciduous woods, on mountain slopes, or in the rich alluvial soil of hollows and coves. The plants are only a few inches tall, with apple-green leaves that arch gracefully from the tiny rhizomes. They spread rapidly by means of runners.

In spring, about the time the Dwarf Bearded Irises bloom, the broad clumps of the Dwarf Crested Iris become sheets of blue. Each flowering stalk bears one to three 1-in.-wide blooms that open flat, like a Japanese Iris (photo, above). Pure white forms (which are not very vigorous) are known, but more usually the color is a light blue-violet, with a deep orange crest. After the plants bloom, the leaves persist until fall, when they slowly turn a pleasing light yellow before withering away.

The Dwarf Crested Iris is quite adaptable. I have seen it growing wild on sunny roadbanks as well as in deep woods, and the amount of flowering seems to depend at least in part on how much sun it gets. The creeping rhizomes are not deeply rooted, so the plants are best moved by lifting "sods" of rhizomes with the soil adhering to them and planting them in shallow excavations previously prepared to receive them. Covered with a light mulch of leaf mold, these clumps will quickly establish themselves if transplanted shortly after flowering, when they make the most active growth.

IRIS LACUSTRIS

Iris lacustris, the Lake Iris, is related to *Iris cristata* but is even more of a dwarf. It is also more prolific than *I. cristata* where it is happy, producing tufted clumps of leaves a few inches high (photo, below left). It is found around the Great Lakes, often growing on granite outcrops, in pockets of acid humus produced by the decay of pine and cedar needles. Like *I. cristata,* it is probably hardy well into USDA Zone 5.

A miniature North American native, *Iris lacustris* can be found in crumbling granite banks around the Great Lakes. Shown above is the rare white form.

The ruffled, lavender blue flowers of *Iris tectorum,* at right, are produced on branched stalks in the early part of the iris season.

IRIS TECTORUM

At the woodland margin and continuing on into full sun, another Crested Iris thrives. This is the well-known *Iris tectorum,* the Roof Iris, so called because in China and Japan it is reputedly planted on roofs to bind the thatch. It is originally native to the Himalayas.

The leaf fans resemble giant versions of those of the Dwarf Crested Iris, with the same pleasing shade of green and the same graceful arching habit. The rhizomes of this iris, though, resemble those of the Bearded Irises, except that they may be green where exposed to the rays of the sun.

Bloomstalks are from 10 in. to 18 in. tall and carry large, flat-opening blooms of lavender blue with a dappling of deeper color (photo at right, facing page). The prominent crest may be white or yellow. There is a lot of variation in plant habit; one type I have raised from seed has three branches and a terminal bud on each bloomstalk. A beautiful white variety, 'Alba,' is well worth seeking out.

Iris tectorum prefers a steady supply of moisture and a soil rich in organic matter. I have read that this iris quickly exhausts the nutrients within reach and so has to be moved and divided often. This has not been the case in my garden; some of my plants have not been disturbed for five years or more and continue to thrive. All that seems to be needed is some new organic matter in the form of leaf mold, added as a light mulch each spring. But if you do want to establish new clumps, the best time to move the plants is just after they bloom. They can be handled much like Bearded Irises. In my garden, *I. tectorum* is a prolific self-seeder as well.

The hybrid 'Paltec' contrasts here with crimson azaleas.

The larger Crested Irises such as the Roof Iris and the rarely available *Iris milesii* bloom with the Tall Bearded Irises and unfortunately seem to share most of their diseases and pests, particularly fungal leaf spot. See p. 52 for what to do should this problem arise.

'PALTEC'

The relationship between the Crested and Bearded irises was established years ago with the appearance of 'Paltec' (photo above), a hybrid between *Iris tectorum* and a variety of the bearded species, *Iris pallida* 'Edina'. This little gem is a vigorous plant in the Northeast, though it seems to have trouble getting through the summers south of Washington, D.C. Like the Roof Iris, 'Paltec' grows about 1 ft. tall, with a well-branched stem carrying typical iris blooms in a satiny light blue. As expected, the flowers have both crest and beard. 'Paltec' makes a wonderful low border for beds of other irises.

IRIS JAPONICA AND *I. WATTII*

To round out a discussion of the Crested Irises, we must include the less hardy members of the clan. *Iris japonica* and *I. wattii* and their relatives are native to southerly regions of China (*japonica* was imported to Japan and discovered there by Western botanists, hence its misleading name) and are not reliable north of USDA Zone 8. I have *I. japonica* in my garden here in central Virginia (Zone 7a) but much of the planting is devastated by winter, and in ten years I have seen only a single bloomstalk.

Iris japonica has frilled and ruffled flowers about 3 in. in diameter, produced in large numbers on branched stems. This is an unusual white-flowering form that may be a hybrid.

Luckily for the iris fanatic, these subtropical Crested Irises grow readily in pots if given plenty of light. In Zone 8 and south, they may be used as ground covers in partially shaded areas, where they will spread rapidly by means of long runners. The flowers are exquisitely beautiful—frilled and ruffled, and in shades of blue, violet, and white (photo, below left).

Iris wattii, when well grown, throws up multiple-branched stalks that may reach a height of 6 ft., with scores of buds. These bamboo-like stems may persist and bloom for more than one season. This plant prefers a soil rich in humus, and in hot regions like Southern California, partial shade.

An Iris for Deep Shade

In truly deep and permanent shade, only one iris will thrive and bloom, and that is a beardless native of Europe, *Iris foetidissima* (photo at left, facing page). In Britain, this pretty plant goes by the name of 'Stinking Gladwyn' or 'Beefsteak Iris', both names referring to the meaty odor of the bruised foliage. In the normal course of events, there is no smell at all, so the names are more than a little unfair. *Iris foetidissima* grows wild in woods and hedgerows throughout England, and in suitable American habitats, it naturalizes. My original planting has spread, by means of scattered seed, through much of the woods on my property.

The scarlet seeds of *Iris foetidissima* contrast with *Achillea* 'Moonshine' in a dried fall arrangement (above). At left, a large clump of *Iris foetidissima* in full bloom along a shady garden path.

The flowers of this iris are not its best point, though they are attractive enough, resembling a small Spuria Iris (and like the Spurias, *I. foetidissima* produces abundant nectar at the base of the falls). Bloom occurs during the Tall Bearded Iris season.

Color ranges from a sort of lavender-tan to violets and pale yellows, but is never very striking. What happens afterwards, if the flowers are pollinated, more than makes up for their drabness. As the frosts of fall approach, the fat seed pods of this iris split open, revealing brilliant scarlet seeds that cling to the wings of the opened pod (photo, above right). They add a great touch to dried or winter arrangements, and stay fresh for two months or more, after which they turn brown and drop from the pod (if this happens out in the garden, abundant seedlings will be the result).

The foliage of *I. foetidissima* is deep green with a blackish overlay, and wonderfully glossy, so that when plants grow close together an aristocratic ground cover results. There is only one problem—the leaves are evergreen and can look battered after a long winter. Writers refer to a variegated form, which would be great in woods, and to varieties with yellow or white seeds. I have never seen any of these in this country, but they might be available in Britain.

Iris foetidissima is reliably hardy at least to USDA Zone 6. It seems to do best under the high shade of deciduous trees in an organic-rich soil, but the more light, the more bloom, and hence the more of those bright and useful seeds. The plant seems relatively immune to diseases and pests, but is attacked from time to time by iris borers (see pp. 54-57).

Pacific Coast Native Irises

For the gardener in the Pacific Northwest and Southern California, Pacific Coast Native Irises (PCNs or PCIs) are ideal plants for lightly shaded woodlands. This group (Series Californicae) contains perhaps a dozen species, all native to the mountains of the Pacific Coast of North America. Species are distributed from the San Francisco Bay Area northward into Oregon. These irises are also popular and well adapted in Britain and Ireland, particularly along the western coasts, where the warm Gulf Stream works its wonders and palms grace the Scottish islands. There have also been many reports of success from suitable regions of Australia and New Zealand.

After many a struggle, and with great regret, I had to give up my attempts to grow Pacific Coast Native Irises, in Virginia. Their requirements for specific conditions seem as stringent, if not more so, than the Aril Irises. Mild winters and long, cool springs, followed by hot, dry, baking summers appear to be necessary, and some of the species and hybrids are not fully hardy. Sharp drainage in a rich but gravelly soil works best. Despite my personal failure, some gardeners in regions as disparate as Arkansas and Michigan are having moderate success with these irises.

IRIS DOUGLASIANA

The Douglas Iris, *Iris douglasiana,* is a robust and widespread species that favors disturbed areas and is often found on bluffs overhanging the

Iris douglasiana **hails from the California coast and may be the most adaptable of the Series Californicae.**

'Big Wheel' is a Pacific Coast Native Iris hybrid.

ocean (I've seen some fine clumps near the piers of the Golden Gate Bridge in San Francisco). With flowers ranging from pure white to deep red-violet (photo at left, facing page), *I. douglasiana* has vigorous, upright foliage and blooms at a height of about 20 in. Growing in a variety of conditions and soils, it's a good species to try if your garden is not within the favored region for these irises.

IRIS INNOMINATA

Many PCNs are lower-growing species that typically are found in mountain meadows and in open forests, where they enjoy the cool partial shade and dappled sunlight. *Iris innominata* is native to a small region of northern California and adjoining Oregon. It is a densely clumping species that blooms at a height of 10 in. to 12 in., and its broad flowers come in an astonishing spectrum of colors, from white to yellow and through pale violet to deep purple. The blooms of the lighter-colored forms are often heavily veined a darker color. Though hardy and a fine garden plant where it is adapted, *I. innominata* seems to require a thorough drying and baking in summer after a wet winter and spring.

IRIS PURDYI AND IRIS TENAX

The Redwood Iris, *Iris purdyi,* is found in northern California; the flowers are yellow with deep purple veining. *I. tenax,* said to be relatively easy to grow, occurs from central Washington to southern Oregon. The single-flowered stems are produced in great profusion; flower color is usually some shade of blue or purple.

NEW HYBRIDS

While the species are well worth growing, they have been eclipsed through the production of hybrids. All of the PCN species are interfertile, and in the wild, natural hybrids can be found wherever two or more species occur together. Taking their cue from this willingness to hybridize, a small but enthusiastic group of breeders has, in only a few decades, wrought changes in the PCN group comparable to those made in the Louisiana Irises. Larger, broader, more ruffled flowers, a wider color range, and a striking expansion of color pattern have been the result (photo at right, facing page). Scores of varieties that far surpass the species are now available from specialty nurseries in the Pacific Northwest and Southern California (see pp. 162-165), as well as in England.

CULTURAL REQUIREMENTS

Plants can be difficult to establish, so growers ship PCNs either in pots or in plastic bags, packed in peat moss. Fall seems to be the preferred planting season, allowing establishment through the winter, when the plants do most of their growing. After blooming, nearly all PCNs will appreciate drying off, and some prefer a period of heat and drought similar to the habitat of their ancestors. However, if drainage is sharp enough, others may stay green through the summer and will not resent watering.

The ideal conditions for Pacific Coast Native Irises would replicate their natural habitat in the partial shade of the evergreen forests, though hybrids raised in Southern California can take more sun. Soil should be slightly acid, organic, and contain enough coarse material (sharp grit or decomposed granite) to allow water to pass through rapidly.

Pacific Coast Native Irises produce abundant seeds, and pods must be picked off or unwanted seedlings will spring up and perhaps overwhelm the clumps of valued named varieties. But there

A USEFUL IRIS RELATIVE

Older books on irises often include the Vesper Iris, then called *Iris dichotoma*. But botanists have decided that this species is too different from the other members of the genus *Iris* to be included any longer, so it has been exiled to a genus of its own and is now properly called *Pardanthopsis dichotoma*. The name Vesper Iris has stuck, though.

The Vesper Iris is a valuable addition to the iris garden for a number of reasons. First of all, it is the last of iris-like plants to bloom, from high summer into the early fall. Second, it is the only one of the group that can be grown as an annual, if preferred; seed started early in February will produce blooming plants late that same summer. Finally, it is one of those rare plants that actually puts on an act in the garden. The flowers open in the early evening over a period of just a minute or two.

With leaf fans typically carried on short, jointed stems and tall, willowy bloomstalks, abundantly branched, that can attain a height of 4 ft., the Vesper Iris is a good choice for a border or for mixing into a planting of real irises for late summer color. The flowers are small, only about 1 in. wide, and indeed look like irises (photo, right). They come in colors from pure white to violet, some with dappling of a darker shade. Each flower begins to open

around five o'clock in the evening, hence the name. By morning the previous day's blooms have curled into tight little spirals, to be replaced later that day by new ones from the profusion of buds.

Pardanthopsis is easily raised from seed (in fact, plants are hard to find). Plant seeds in pots or flats as soon as they are available and stratify them (see p. 149 for an explanation of this process). After coming out of cold

No longer considered a true iris, the Vesper Iris (*Pardanthopsis dichotoma*) still has its place in the iris garden.

storage, the seeds will germinate in a week or two. Transplant the seedlings and keep them growing rapidly if blooming that summer is a goal. Set out plants in the garden from 4-in. pots when the weather permits. Full sun is ideal, in a fertile loamy soil. The Vesper Iris is not a long-lived perennial, and most plants will live only three or four years, eventually making a small clump of a dozen or so fans. Keep new plants coming on from seed to replace the old ones that die out.

As a measure of its distinctiveness, *Pardanthopsis dichotoma* has never been successfully crossed with a real iris, but does form hybrids with the yellow or orange Blackberry Lily, *Belamcanda*. Samuel Norris of Kentucky developed a particularly attractive strain of these hybrids, which were given the name × *Pardancanda norrisi*. (The × in front of the name indicates a hybrid between different genera.) Seeds of these plants, sold as 'Candy Lilies', are available from some of the major seed houses. They are attractive plants with a very wide range of colors and patterns. However, the original strain had flowers that were more iris-like, and the presently available seed produces blooms like multicolored *Belamcanda*. Perhaps back-crossing to the Vesper Iris would restore their original charm. Grow them just as described for *Pardanthopsis*.

Above, the white and yellow Calsibe hybrid 'Lyric Laughter'.

Often found growing under pines, *Iris verna*, right, likes an acid soil.

is an upside to this—the plants can easily be grown from seed, and seed is often available in quantity from PCN growers. A strategy that has produced some results for enthusiasts in other parts of North America has been to grow hundreds of seedlings in the hope of finding a few that are adapted to local conditions. It's a grand experiment that with a little luck could have stunning results.

The range of adaptability of the PCN Irises has been somewhat improved by crossing them with members of the 40-chromosome Chrysographes group of the Siberian Irises. These lovely plants, called Calsibes (photo, above left), are worth a try.

Iris verna

Finally, a woodland iris for the gardener in the eastern and midwestern sections of North America. The Vernal Iris, *Iris verna,* is often found growing not far from the Dwarf Crested Iris, but the Vernal Iris has more "iris-like" flowers, with erect standards. Its 1-in.-high light blue-violet flowers are carried on long, delicate tubes at a height of about 6 in. (photo, above right). The foliage is much narrower, more erect, and a darker green than that of the Dwarf Crested Iris.

Not much is available on the culture of the Vernal Iris; I can only report my own experience. Plants set out in November among azaleas and pines, in a sandy acid soil, have succeeded mightily, making large clumps over the years, but rhizomes planted at the same time in moist humus in deciduous woods failed. So perhaps *Iris verna* is a good choice for the piney woods of the middle South!

An Iris that Blooms in Winter

English gardeners have long been enthusiastic about the Winter Iris, *Iris unguicularis* (photo, below); I think it may have something to do with the English fascination with the Mediterranean and the Greek Islands, for it is there (and North Africa as well) that the Winter Iris is native. Or perhaps it might be the sudden appearance, often undetected until fully open, of the bright blooms nestled in the foliage, spreading a sweet fragrance all around. This iris blooms when other flowers are scarce, any time from October to March.

The Winter Iris is a low-growing plant, with 1-ft.-long leaves springing from small, gnarled rhizomes. The blooms are carried singly on long tubes a few inches tall (the flowers are in fact stemless), and often the foliage must be parted to enjoy them fully. The color range is from pure white (rare) to lavender blue and purple.

Winter-blooming *Iris unguicularis*.

Some varieties (e.g., 'Winter Goldback') have the backs of the falls brushed or dusted with deep yellow. Most varieties are very fragrant. A wide range of named forms is available in Britain, but only a few are available in North America.

The Winter Iris is particularly successful in southern California and coastal Western Australia, two places where the climate is essentially similar to the plants' native Mediterranean habitat. However, it is also a garden staple in Britain, and more and more North American gardeners are finding it adaptable. You will have to try it to see if it will grow in the garden for you; just now I'm keeping mine in pots that go outside in summer. In winter, they need only be protected against a hard freeze, even when about to bloom. A few miles away, in the garden of Mike and Anne Lowe, large clumps of several *I. unguicularis* varieties flourish outdoors in a sheltered spot.

At least a few varieties can survive temperatures in the single digits with a little snow protection, but temperatures that low would destroy the flower buds. Some gardeners recommend keeping a cardboard box handy when the plants begin to bloom; it can be used to cover them at night. I'd recommend two boxes—a small one over the plants and then a larger box over the small one. The layer of air trapped between them will be an effective insulator.

CULTURE IN THE GROUND

To grow *I. unguicularis* out-of-doors, select a warm, sunny spot in the rock garden, between boulders that will warm the air and soil on sunny winter days. Another good spot would be up against a south-facing foundation wall, where crumbling mortar might also create the slightly alkaline conditions the Winter Iris likes. Keep things on the dry side during the summer, but make sure of abundant water in spring.

CONTAINER CULTURE

The Winter Iris responds well to container culture. Soil should be gritty and well drained, but it need not be highly fertile. Water the plants well during the late winter and spring, but keep them rather dry through the summer and fall. So long as the soil in the pot does not freeze, the plants should be fine. I keep mine in an unheated garage. Check for blooms beginning in late January and bring the pots into the house to enjoy them in comfort.

GROWING YOUR OWN IRISES

Iris Seeds

Growing Irises from Seed

Trying Your Hand at Hybridizing

Gardeners who delight in the challenge of growing plants from seed will sooner or later want to try with irises. With very few exceptions, irises are easily grown from seed, and the rewards for your labors are great. If you enjoy the experience of a morning walk in your garden at iris time, reveling in the new blooms of the varieties purchased the previous year, you'll find the excitement at a whole new level when the new flowers are produced by your own seedlings.

Those who become real enthusiasts for this most diverse of modern perennials may even want to undertake a modest hybridizing program of their own. This is truly creative gardening—not just planning and designing using known plants, but an exploration of the unknown, creating plants that have never before existed and that are unique in all the world to your very own garden.

Iris Seeds

Iris seeds form in seed pods (photo, below right). The seeds themselves are large and easy to handle; most types provide no challenge, even to the beginning gardener. Like other seeds, they have three basic components: a tough outer **seed coat,** enclosed stored food, or **endosperm,** to nourish the young seedling, and finally the young plant, or **embryo,** itself.

In fresh seed, the coat is often taut and shiny, but as the seed dries, the endosperm loses water and the seed coat wrinkles. This is no cause for alarm but is a natural process. The drying makes it possible for the embryo to enter dormancy, a state of suspended animation. Dormant seeds can live for years if necessary, until the proper conditions for **germination,** or sprouting, occur. Seeds of some types of iris, such as Arils, can remain viable for at least up to ten years; the seeds of other types are not so long-lived.

The dormant state that dried seeds enter is induced by substances in the seed coat and endosperm called **germination inhibitors.** Inhibitors are commonly found in the seeds of most perennial plants, and their function is to keep the seeds from germinating at inappropriate times, when the survival of the seedlings would be in question. Before the seed can germinate, the inhibitors must be washed out or neutralized, which can best be done by a process known as **stratification.** This will occur naturally if you plant your seeds outdoors in the garden in late fall. Autumn rains and the water from melting snow will leach the inhibitors from the seeds, allowing them to sprout in the spring. The process is enhanced by cool or cold temperatures (around 40°F or below) for at least six weeks. If you plant your seeds indoors, you must stratify them artificially, as described on p. 149.

Not all iris seeds look the same. Bearded Irises have rich brown seeds, which, when fresh, have a shiny seed coat. Upon drying, however, the seed coat becomes wrinkled as the endosperm loses water and shrinks. Long-lived Aril Iris seeds have a white or cream-colored knob, the aril, on each seed. The seed coats of Louisiana Irises have an extra layer that is thick and corky, so that the seeds float and can be dispersed by moving water. *Iris prismatica,* a North American native, is called the Cube-seeded Iris, for the shape of its seeds.

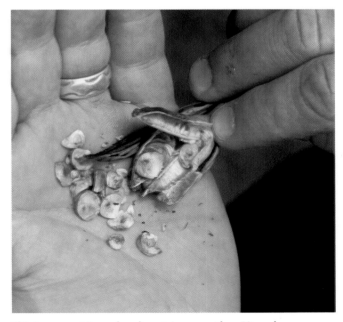

This Japanese Iris seed pod contains more than 50 seeds.

Growing Irises
from Seed

You can obtain iris seeds from friends or through mail order. Perhaps the most extensive seed list available is that of SIGNA, the Species Iris Group of North America. Literally hundreds of species and varieties of every kind of iris (and a generous selection of iris relatives) are offered annually to members at a bargain price—as of this writing, $0.50 a packet. You must be a member to receive the list; see p. 158 for information on how to join.

Commercial seed catalogs usually list only a few iris varieties or species for sale (an exception is a Michigan outfit, Arrowhead Alpines, which sells more than 60 different kinds—see p. 163 for the address).

A third, and more adventurous, way to obtain seed is to produce your own through hybridization (see pp. 152-157).

Seed ordered through the mail will most likely arrive looking wrinkled and sere. The packet may include a certain amount of chaff or of inviable seeds, which usually can easily be distinguished from the viable ones. However, I always plant them all, on the chance that even the smallest, most wrinkled-looking seed might germinate and produce a world-beating plant!

PLANTING SEEDS OUTDOORS

Seeds may be planted in rows outdoors in a sunny protected spot. The soil should be prepared much as for a bed to be planted with iris rhizomes (see pp. 40-41), and tilled and raked until all clods have been broken and a fine, level surface is achieved. Plant the seeds at least 1 in. apart and at a depth three to four times their diameter. Deeper planting, up to 1 in., is sometimes recommended for very cold climates, where alternating freezes and thaws might heave the seeds out of the ground if they were planted too shallow.

Seed rows should be carefully marked (photo, left). Don't rely on your all-too-fallible memory to recall where the seed rows are and what was planted there! Seed beds can be mulched for the winter with the lightest and airiest of materials. Pay special attention to the task of removing the mulch in spring; it must be done carefully, so that the seeds are not disturbed.

Rows of iris seedlings in the North Carolina garden of hybridizer Lloyd Zurbrigg.

STARTING SEEDS INDOORS

If you prefer to avoid the vagaries of fall and winter weather, as I do, you can start your iris seeds indoors in a greenhouse, sun room, or even on a bright windowsill. Starting seeds in pots can help short-season gardeners in that the young plants can be germinated weeks before garden-planted seed, giving the irises extra time to make good plants their first summer.

The potting soil

Plant the seeds in November in a standard commercial potting mix. Such a mix has an one big advantage over soil you might get from your garden: It has been sterilized and will contain no disease organisms. If you insist on using your own soil, you will need to sterilize it. I've had success microwaving small batches of damp soil mix on high for about 10 minutes, but others who share your house might object strenuously both to the smell of cooking soil and the use of a kitchen appliance for such a purpose! You can consult your local extension agent for other alternatives.

The pots

Ccontainers for seed starting can be of various types, but they should have drainage holes in the bottom and they should be scrupulously clean. Cleanliness is essential to protect the seedlings from disease organisms—chiefly damping-off fungus (see p. 150). Plastic pots are preferable because they are easy to sterilize: Wash them thoroughly with soap and water, then rinse them with a solution of one part chlorine bleach to nine parts of water and let them dry completely. Clay pots are not as good a choice because they are riddled with microscopic pores in which disease organisms can hide from the sterilization process. If you insist on using clay pots, they must be heat sterilized. After a thorough washing, place the pots, soaking wet, in a 350°F oven for 30 minutes. Disposable fiber-based flats do not need sterilizing, but should be used only once. Reusable wooden flats are not recommended because they are too difficult to sterilize.

Planting

Up to 20 iris seeds can be planted in a 4-in. pot, provided you transplant the seedlings before they become too crowded. Seeds may be planted in pots at the same depth you would plant them outdoors. Be sure the soil in each pot is thoroughly moistened, but there should be no dripping from the drainage holes.

Stratification

After carefully labeling the pots, place each in a plastic bag and put the bags into an old refrigerator used for just this purpose, adjusted to between 35°F and 40°F. (I don't recommend using your kitchen refrigerator because fruit stored there gives off ethylene gas, a plant hormone that can damage seeds.) Leave the pots in the refrigerator for six weeks so the seeds can undergo the process of stratification, just as they might if they had been planted outside.

Light

Iris seedlings require the brightest possible light. In dim light, the seedlings will become weak and spindly, and the whole purpose of an early start will be defeated. A compromise method used successfully by many iris enthusiasts is to plant the seeds in pots, but then put the pots outdoors. They must not be allowed to freeze solid, however, and should be kept under a pile of mulch or in a cold frame.

WHEN THE SEEDS SPROUT

When weather warms in spring, watch for the tiny green spears of the new seedlings emerging above ground level. Each small seedling will remain linked to its seed (which stays under the ground) by an umbilicus-like structure called a **cotyledon.** This allows the plant to continue to withdraw food from the endosperm and so grow rapidly to a self-supporting size. Within a few weeks, the seedlings will reach a height of 4 in. to 6 in. At this stage they will have exhausted the reserves in the seed, have good root systems, and be living and growing on the food produced in their own leaves.

Potted seedlings, and to a lesser extent those grown in the ground, may be attacked by a soil-borne fungus disease called **damping-off,** which causes the young seedlings to rot at soil level and fall over. Damping-off can run through a pot of seedlings at lightning speed, and even seeds potted in sterile mix are not immune—airborne spores can infect the pots afterwards. The disease is almost a certainty if seeds are potted in unsterilized garden soil. At the earliest sign, drench the pot with a systemic fungicide; this should handle the problem and stop the fungus in its tracks.

TRANSPLANTING YOUR SEEDLINGS

Whether they are grown in pots or started outdoors, the more robust seedlings will crowd and inhibit their less rugged neighbors. Young seedlings should be transplanted to a permanent position before they become so crowded as to interfere with one another (photos, facing page). The nursery bed for the seedlings' first year should be prepared just as for a planting of iris rhizomes, but with special attention to maintaining the fine tilth of the soil. Your young seedlings have rather small root systems that will be set back by transplanting. Fine soil, without large clods, will allow these roots to come in contact with soil moisture and not find themselves in spaces between soil clods, where they will be likely to dry out.

Even though transplanting is a shock to the roots of seedlings, cutting back the foliage, as you would do while transplanting mature irises, is not recommended; this would shock them even more and prolong their recovery. It is wise to do the transplanting on an overcast day, or even a drizzly one. On sunny days, the young plants will lose a great deal of moisture from their leaves, moisture that the disturbed root system will be hard pressed to make up. If you must transplant on a sunny day, wait until evening so the cool, humid night will give the plants some respite.

Spacing of the seedlings in the nursery bed will differ according to the type of iris. For Tall Bearded Irises, the likely subject of your first experiments, at least 1 ft. apart is recommended. Types that might take longer to reach blooming size, such as Louisianas, Japanese Irises, and Siberian Irises, should be set out farther apart, perhaps as much as 18 in.

The transplants will grow rapidly. Be particularly alert for foliage diseases (see pp. 51-53) on Bearded Iris transplants, as they can slow growth considerably by robbing the plants of leaf surface with which to make food. By the time the new plants' first autumn comes, they should be robust and on a par with freshly divided established plants. The decision as to whether to provide some form of winter protection is yours—follow whatever practice you use for other iris plants of the same type.

1.

2.

3.

FROM POT TO PLOT

1. **Potted iris seedlings after one transplanting are ready to be moved to the garden. These are seedlings of *Iris virginica*.**

2. **The seedlings are separated for transplantation into a nursery bed outdoors.**

3. **Finely tilled soil is firmed around the roots of the newly transplanted seedlings.**

WHEN THE SEEDLINGS FIRST BLOOM

Bearded Iris seedlings that have been treated well will often bloom the next spring after germination. By late summer, those seedlings that are preparing to bloom the following spring will usually show two or more smaller leaf fans on either side of the main fan; these increases will be the blooming rhizomes of two years hence. For other iris types, the wait for bloom may be longer. Most beardless types will need another summer's growth, though a few scattered blooms may occur. Aril Irises and bulbous sorts often require extra time; in particular the bulbous irises may not bloom for as much as five years.

When the foliage of bulbous seedlings dies down, the bulbs may have to be lifted and stored in a warm place to provide the required period of summer dormancy. This can be difficult because the first season bulbs are very small—pea sized at the largest. Search for them carefully when digging!

Trying Your Hand at Hybridizing

With their large, simple flowers, irises are very easy for even a beginner to hybridize. But before rushing out to the garden to make some crosses, consider carefully. Planned crosses almost always provide better results than ones made at random or impulsively. Choose parents that already exhibit qualities you would like to see in your seedlings, such as vigor, disease resistance, and habit typical for the kind of iris, and, of course, attractive form and color. Inferior parents will rarely produce a superior offspring. It is only through selecting outstanding parents for crosses that the rare individual will be obtained that may exceed them both in desirability.

Even with the most careful selection of parents, you must prepare yourself for disappointment. The genetics of irises are complex, and the best qualities are not always passed on to offspring. Geneticists have long been aware of a phenomenon called **regression to the mean,** in which the offspring of outstanding parents have a tendency to drop back in many of their characteristics to the average for the population as a whole. It is well to remember the vegetable breeders who crossed radishes and cabbages (which are actually quite closely related plants), hoping for radish-rooted plants that would bear cabbages above ground. What they got, unfortunately, was plants with cabbage roots and radish tops.

A long and detailed treatise on iris genetics is beyond the scope of this book. For an excellent introduction to the subject, readers can consult *The World of Irises,* edited by Bee Warburton and Melba Hamblen (see p. 167).

GETTING STARTED

You won't have to invest in specialized equipment, but you will need a few items before you begin. A small pair of forceps or tweezers is the tool of choice for collecting the pollen-bearing anthers. You may also need some small glass or plastic vials or tubes to store the anthers in, and tie-on paper labels for tagging the pollinated blooms and for connecting the seed pod you hope will form with the notes you have taken recording the parentage (see the sidebar on p. 154)—and for that you'll need pencils and a notebook. You will also appreciate having a box, tray, or other container to hold your gear and make it easy to carry everything into the garden. Some professionals prefer to use an apron with many commodious pockets, or a fisherman's vest.

POLLINATING THE PLANTS

Once you have selected the first parents for your new hybridizing program and assembled your gear, you are ready to go into the garden and actually make the crosses. Let's assume for now that you are going to work with Tall Bearded Irises. If you will be working with

Making the cross

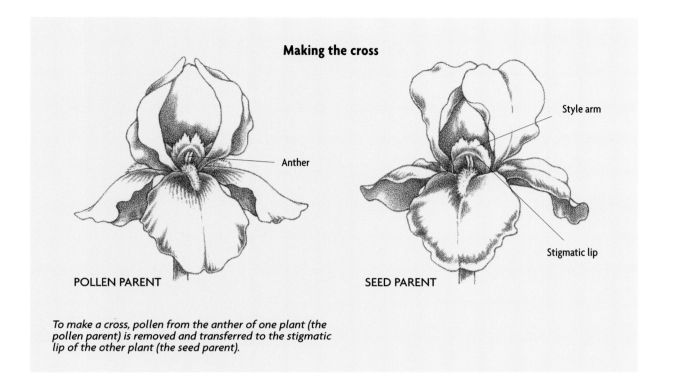

POLLEN PARENT

Anther

SEED PARENT

Style arm

Stigmatic lip

To make a cross, pollen from the anther of one plant (the pollen parent) is removed and transferred to the stigmatic lip of the other plant (the seed parent).

beardless types, there are a few things you'll need to do differently; these are discussed on pp. 156-157.

Once in the garden, the two parts of the iris flower that you must be able to distinguish are the pollen-bearing **anthers** and the **stigmatic lip,** which receives pollen. These structures are close together in the floral anatomy (drawing, above), the stigmatic lip near the tip of the style arm, and the anther attached to the base of the bloom, tucked in beneath the style arm. The variety or species that will contribute the pollen for the cross is called the **pollen parent,** while the one that will develop the seeds is the **seed parent.** For most kinds of irises, a plant can play either role, but in a few cases, some types may be either pollen sterile or seed sterile, or both.

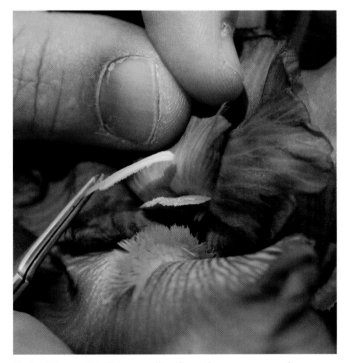

To fertilize an iris flower, pollen from the same or another variety is applied to the stigmatic lip of the style arm.

The fertility of a particular plant can be ascertained only through experience with the plants themselves.

Now examine the anthers of the pollen parent carefully. If they are mature and producing pollen, you will be able to see a yellow, white, or bluish powder adhering to them. It usually takes at least a few hours after a flower first opens for the anthers to mature, open, and show their pollen.

Making the cross could not be simpler. Using forceps or tweezers, remove one of the anthers from a bloom of the pollen parent. Select a bloom on the seed parent that has been open for one day or less. If the seed-parent plant is nearby, you can simply carry the anther there. Then, after pulling back the crests of style arms with thumb and forefinger to expose the stigmatic lip, wipe some of the pollen from the anther on to the lip (photo, p. 153). It may take some hours after the bloom first opens for the stigmatic lip to become receptive, but even if pollen is placed on a not-quite-ready stigmatic lip, it will effect fertilization when the proper time comes. Although placing pollen on just one stigmatic lip is probably sufficient to produce a full pod of seeds, it is wise to pollinate all three stigmatic lips on the flower as insurance.

Often, pollen parents and seed parents do not bloom at the same time. If the pollen parent blooms first, anthers can be collected in small vials or tubes stoppered with cotton, which can be stored in the refrigerator until the seed parent blooms. If the seed parent blooms first, an iris grower in a more southerly region might have the pollen parent already in bloom. Pollen can be shaken off into an envelope and sent through the mail without evident harm. The pollen then can be removed from the envelope and transferred to the seed parent's stigmatic lip using a small water-color brush.

THE IMPORTANCE OF KEEPING CAREFUL RECORDS

Good recordkeeping is extraordinarily important, even if only a few crosses are made just for fun. In your notebook, identify each cross you make with a code number you assign. For example, the first cross you make in 1999 might be called 99-1 in your notebook. Opposite the code number, record the parents. By convention, the name of the seed parent precedes the name of the pollen parent; the × separating the two names indicates the hybridization. For example, if cross 99-1 is 'Stepping Out' × 'Victoria Falls', we know that pollen of 'Victoria Falls' was placed on the stigma of 'Stepping Out'.

Attach a tag bearing the code number of the cross to the seed parent's bloomstalk just below the ovary. Remember that this tag is going to be exposed to the weather all summer, so select one that will last, and write on it with pencil or water-proof marker, not with a soluble or fading ink.

Not all attempted crosses will result in seeds (see the discussion on the facing page), so it's a good idea to leave space in your notebook for recording whether a pod formed, and if so, how many seeds it contained. When you plant any seeds that have formed, write down that number as well, and in the spring make note of the number of seedlings that appear. Then assign each seedling an additional number, such as 99-1-7, the seventh seedling of the first cross in 1999.

Partially mature iris seed pods are green. The pods at right are formed on plants of *Iris tectorum*. Mature iris seed pods turn brown and crack open at the top (far right). Collect the pods quickly at this stage, or you risk losing the seeds.

Pollen grains are too small to see with the naked eye, and unbeknownst to you, a few may adhere to the brushes or vials used to transfer or store them. So before using them for another cross, thoroughly wash such implements—you wouldn't want pollen from the wrong parent to effect fertilization. Some hybridizers use toothpicks or matchsticks to transfer pollen and throw them away after use.

WATCHING FOR RESULTS

Within about three days of pollination, if you used a fresh flower of the seed parent, the ovary of the pollinated bloom will enlarge slightly, indicating that perhaps the cross was successful. Be careful not to snap off any pollinated flowers; the process of fertilization may take some time after pollen transfer. The pollen grains must sprout and send a long, hollow tube down through the stigmatic tissues. In the ovary, these tubes eventually reach the **ovules,**

or potential seeds, and fertilize them. Only fertilized ovules will become seeds. Warn garden visitors not to be "helpful" in snapping off spent blooms!

After several more days have passed, if the cross was unsuccessful, the ovary will shrivel, turn yellow, and drop off. If the cross was successful, the ovary containing developing seeds will become noticeably larger. Successful seed pods will grow larger through the summer, eventually turning yellow or brown and cracking open at the top (photos, above). (Rarely, a pod will be completely empty, what experts call a **balloon.**) If the exposed seeds are brown and glossy, they are ready for harvest. Collect the seeds in an envelope, and label it with the number you gave the cross in your notebook. Then sow the seeds and care for them as described on pp. 148-152.

PREVENTING UNWANTED POLLINATION

In the natural course of events, Tall Bearded Irises rarely form seed pods. When pods full of seeds do appear spontaneously in Tall Bearded Iris plantings, it's because insects have carried pollen from one flower to another or by some manner of means, pollen from the same flower has reached the stigmatic lip. Of course, the pollen parent is unknown for such crosses, but it is up to you to decide to keep or discard the seeds.

Iris hybridizers Dave Niswonger (in cap) and Rick Ernst inspect a field of Tall Bearded Iris seedlings at Cooley's Gardens in Oregon. Nearly all these seedlings will be discarded because they show no improvement over their parents.

The appearance of these chance pods raises the question of insects bringing additional pollen to a seed-parent bloom either just before or just after you have pollinated it yourself. Experience suggests that this is not very likely, at least for Tall Bearded Irises. Their blooms are so large and so constructed that insect pollination can be effected only by the largest bumblebees. However, just to be on the safe side, many professionals take the precaution of breaking off the fall petals of pollinated flowers so bumblebees will not have a landing platform. Others pop a small paper bag over the pollinated bloom until they are sure the cross has taken. (The bags could be counterproductive on windy days, though, because the flower could be snapped off before fertilization occurs.)

SPECIAL PRECAUTIONS FOR BEARDLESS IRISES

In contrast to the Tall Bearded Irises, many beardless forms, especially the Siberians, self-pollinate readily or can easily be pollinated by bees. Left totally alone, almost every flower in a clump of Siberian Irises will form a seed pod, usually as a result of visits from bees.

While crosses of all types of irises can be made by the methods described above, you must take special precautions with beardless irises to avoid unwanted pollination before and after you make your cross. The method described by Currier McEwen for Siberians in his book *The Siberian Iris* (see p. 167) will work for all beardless irises. Briefly, here's what to do: Select as a seed parent a flower in the early stages of opening and carefully unfold the petals. At this point, the pollen will be far from mature, so the anthers can be safely removed and discarded. Using a strip of foliage, tie up the falls so that

The odds of raising a commercially successful iris hybrid are very slim. Premier iris breeder Ray Schreiner says he selects from among 10,000 seedlings raised annually only 15 for further testing, and of those, only two or three might eventually find their way into catalogs. Just because of numbers, the pros have a crucial edge. But once in a great while, a rank amateur wins the hybridizing sweepstakes.

One of these rare winners was a Midwesterner named Lois Kuntz, who had grown Tall Bearded Irises in her backyard for years. In the late 1950s, she decided to try her luck at making a cross. Selecting two pink-flowered varieties impulsively, she got a single pod and a handful of seeds, which she planted. The following spring, about 20 seedlings emerged, and most of them bloomed a year later. Disappointed in the "muddy pink" colors, she discarded them all except the last to bloom, a beautifully ruffled cream and yellow

'Debby Rairdon', a humble backyard hybrid, was awarded the Dykes Medal, irisdom's most coveted prize.

(photo, above). At the urging of visitors to her garden, she named the new iris 'Debby Rairdon', after one of her grandchildren, eight years old at the time.

'Debby Rairdon' was formally introduced to gardeners in 1965, one of more than 800 varieties registered that year with the American Iris Society, and a year later it won an Honorable Mention Award from the Society. The next step in the AIS award system is the Award of Merit, then given to a dozen irises annually; only AM winners were eligible for the Dykes Medal, the top prize. 'Debby Rairdon' won its AM in 1968, and only three years later was the Dykes Medalist for 1971. As I write this, in 1998, 'Debby Rairdon' still appears on the AIS Popularity Poll, ranking 69th, up from 76th in 1997.

In 1978, Lois Kuntz told writer J. D. Foraker that she regretted not having taken up the offer of a percentage of the profits from the commercial nursery that first sold 'Debby Rairdon'. Instead she received $150 in cash and $150 in iris rhizomes. When Foraker interviewed her, her garden had mostly been converted to lawn. The only iris she was growing was 'Debby Rairdon'.

the flower remains inaccessible to insects. After some hours (or no more than a day), the stigmatic lips will have become receptive, the falls can be untied, and the bloom can be pollinated by hand. Afterwards, either remove the falls or retie them to deter insect visits.

THE MOMENT OF TRUTH

The most difficult task of hybridizing comes when your seedlings bloom. Unless you have unlimited space to preserve them all, you must ruthlessly select only those that are improvements over their parents and get rid of the rest (photo, facing page). Perhaps you will be lucky enough to raise a seedling that will achieve public acclaim, be introduced to commerce, and win top awards from the American Iris Society (see the sidebar above). Or, like most of us, you may only reap the satisfaction of having participated in an act of artistic creation in which the medium is a living, growing plant.

The American Iris Society

Founded in 1920, The American Iris Society (AIS) is dedicated to promoting the culture and improvement of the iris. The AIS publishes a quarterly, color-illustrated *Bulletin* that features articles about iris culture, personalities, the merits of various iris cultivars, and reports of meetings. Each issue also contains a commercial directory, and in the January and April issues, the major hybridizers advertise their new introductions and tout their catalogs.

Administratively, the AIS divides the USA and Canada into 24 regions, each with a Regional Vice President. Within each region are both affiliated and nonaffiliated local clubs and societies; one is almost certainly near you. In addition to the regional organization, there are Sections that cater to people interested in particular kinds of irises. Peculiarly, there is no Section for Tall Bearded Irises, but in 1997, a Tall Bearded Iris Society was organized as a cooperating society of the AIS. This group hopes to publish a newsletter on a regular basis.

The Sections are: Median Iris Society, Dwarf Iris Society, Society for Siberian Irises, Spuria Iris Society, Society for Japanese Irises, Reblooming Iris Society, Society for Pacific Coast Native Irises, Species Iris Group of North America, and the Historic Iris Preservation Society. The Aril Society International and the Society for Louisiana Irises are "cooperating societies" that are organized independently of AIS; one can be a member of these latter two without joining AIS.

An annual individual AIS membership in 1998 cost only $18, a real bargain. As of this writing, the membership secretary is Marilyn Harlow, PO Box 55, Freedom, CA 95019-0055.

The AIS Awards

Recommending iris varieties that will do well in all parts of North America would be an almost impossible task. Instead, I've decided to fall back on a formal alternative, the American Iris Society's awards system and Symposium. For further recommendations, gardeners should join the American Iris Society and contact the organization in their region, or the section that specializes in the particular kind of iris that interests them.

No list of varieties can substitute for actually seeing irises in bloom and assessing for yourself how well they do in your area. On pp. 162-165 you will find a list of iris nurseries (by no means complete); one may be near you. Practically all of them are open to visitors during the bloom season. Visiting an iris nursery is an excellent opportunity to do some comparison shopping.

The top awards for irises are represented by a series of medals for each category. The medals are voted by certified judges of the AIS; judges are expected to vote only for varieties they have personally seen growing in gardens or displayed at iris shows.

The award tiers begin with High Commendation (HC), the first award an iris can win. This award is often given to unnamed seedlings as a signal to the hybridizer that the variety should be considered for introduction. "Introduction" means something very specific—the variety must be registered by name with the AIS and offered to the public for sale, through listing in a grower's catalog or by means of an advertisement in the AIS Bulletin.

One year after being introduced to commerce, a variety is eligible for the next level of recognition, the Honorable Mention (HM). At least 35 judges' votes are required for a Tall Bearded Iris; other classes require fewer votes. Irises that have won an Honorable Mention become eligible for the Award of Merit (AM). The top three or four AM winners usually poll over 100 votes each from the judges. Winning an AM is a prerequisite to being considered for the various medals.

The top award of all is the Dykes Memorial Medal, given to only a single variety annually and named in memory of William Dykes, a great British authority on irises who lived and worked in the early decades of this century. One each of these medals is awarded in North America, Britain, and Australia/New Zealand. Bearded varieties have invariably been the American winners, but Siberians and a single Calsibe hybrid have won the British Dykes.

The other medals are awarded to AM winners by category. (Only one variety can win each year.) The chart on pp. 160-161 gives the winners of the several medals for the past 11 years, working backward from 1997.

The AIS Symposium

The AIS Symposium, published in January in the *Bulletin of the American Iris Society,* has a broader reach; any AIS member is available to vote on a ballot that contains the names of the irises that made the top 100 in the previous year, plus space for write-ins. Only Tall Bearded Irises are considered. In order to get on the Symposium, an iris must be widely available and likely to do well in most parts of the country. However, while the members are urged to vote only for irises they have personally seen, some may vote based on reputation or a catalog photograph.

A list of the top 20 Tall Bearded Irises of 1998 appears at right. Of these, the most durable is 'Stepping Out', a 1968 Dykes Medal winner that was introduced in 1964. It may well become the most popular iris of all time, and it advanced two ranks from the 1997 poll. 'Winter Olympics', at number 74, is the only iris on the list that is older than 'Stepping Out'. The two most recent introductions in the top 20, 'Thornbird' and 'Before the

Storm', were first made available to the public in 1989. Of the entire list of 100 varieties, only 12 were introduced in 1990 or later; three 1994 varieties are the most recent. Thus the Symposium represents well-tested varieties that probably can succeed over wide regions of North America. Nine of the top 20 were hybridized and introduced by Schreiner's Gardens, of Salem, Oregon.

THE IRIS HIT PARADE

The following is a list of the 20 most popular Tall Bearded Irises of 1998, according to the AIS Symposium:

1. Dusky Challenger
2. Silverado
3. Jesse's Song
4. Beverly Sills
5. Vanity
6. Titan's Glory
7. Honky Tonk Blues
8. Stepping Out
9. Edith Wolford
10. Before the Storm
11. Laced Cotton
12. Thornbird
13. Lady Friend
14. Mary Frances
15. Victoria Falls
16. Song of Norway
17. Going My Way
18. Supreme Sultan
19. Sky Hooks
20. Superstition

AMERICAN IRIS SOCIETY MEDAL WINNERS

Award	Category	1997	1996	1995	1994
Dykes Memorial Medal		Thornbird	Before the Storm	Honky Tonk Blues	Silverado
John C. Wister Medal (first awarded in 1993)	Tall Bearded Iris	Acoma	Thornbird	Before the Storm	Honky Tonk Blues
Williamson-White Medal	Miniature Tall Bearded Iris	Zula	Petite Money	Frosted Velvet	Rosemary's Dream
Knowlton Medal	Border Bearded Iris	Sonja's Selah	Lenora Pearl	Calico Cat	Zinger
Hans and Jacob Sass Medal	Intermediate Bearded Iris	Hot Spice	Lemon Pop	Blue Eyed Blonde	Ask Alma
Cook-Douglas Medal	Standard Dwarf Bearded Iris	Bedford Lilac	Pumpin' Iron	Serenity Prayer	Orange Tiger
Caparne-Welch Medal	Miniature Dwarf Bearded Iris	Grapelet	Cinnamon Apples	Spot of Tea	Funny Face
Morgan-Wood Medal	Siberian Iris	Coronation Anthem	Shaker's Prayer	Aqua Whispers	Sultan's Ruby
Mary Swords Deballion Medal	Louisiana Iris	Voo Doo Magic	Professor Jim	Kay Nelson	Jeri
J. A. Payne Medal	Japanese Iris	Electric Rays/ Iapetus (tie)	Edge of Frost/ Kalamazoo (tie)	Cascade Crest	Caprician Butterfly
Eric Nies Medal	Spuria Iris	Countess Zeppelin	Chocolate Fudge	Cinnamon Stick	Son of Sun
C. G. White Medal	Aril (½ Aril or more)	Turkish Pendant	Syrian Princess	Persian Padishah	Khyber Pass
William Mohr Medal	Arilbred (¼ to ½ Aril)	Omar the Tentmaker	Solomon's Glory	Smoke with Wine	Omar's Torch
Sydney B. Mitchell Medal	Pacific Coast Native Iris	Night Editor	Idylwild	Sierra Dell	(no award)

1993	1992	1991	1990	1989	1988	1987
Edith Wolford	Dusky Challenger	Everything Plus	Jesse's Song	(no award)	Titan's Glory	(no award)
Silverado						
Bumblebee Delite	Welch's Reward	Crystal Ruffles	Bumblebee Delite	Little Paul	Aachen Elf	Abridged Version
Zinc Pink	Batik	Shenanigan	Miss Nellie	Peccadillo	Soft Spoken	Drum Solo
Maui Moonlight	Hot Fudge	Butter Pecan	Hellcat	Honey Glazed	Oklahoma Bandit	Az Ap
Dark Vader	Sun Doll	Chubby Cheeks	(no award)	Baby Blessed	Raspberry Jam	Little Black Belt
Sparky	Chubby Cherub	Puppet Baby	Pussytoes	Alpine Lake	Ditto	Gizmo
Jewelled Crown	Lady Vanessa	Mabel Coday	King of Kings	Dance Ballerina Dance	Pink Haze	Steve Varner
Frank Chowning	Bajazzo	Rhett	Acadian Miss	Black Gamecock	Easter Tide	Clara Goula
Oriental Eyes	Japanese Pinwheel	Lilac Peaks	Caprician Butterfly	Blueberry Rimmed	Oriental Eyes	Freckled Geisha
Betty Cooper	Dress Circle	Highline Coral	Cinnamon Stick	Destination	Janice Chesnik	Son of Sun
Syrian Jewel	(no award)	Syrian Jewel	Dee Mouse	Pro News	Tabriz	Cool Oasis
Jewel of Omar	Omar's Torch	Jewel of Omar	Bold Sentry	Green Eyed Sheba	Humohr	Sultan's Jewelry
Mimsey	Mimsey	Drive You Wild	Big Money	California Mystique	(no award)	Simply Wild

IRIS SPECIALIST NURSERIES

Iris specialist nurseries are found in every region of the United States and Canada, but with a definite concentration in California and Oregon and in the Midwest. This list of iris vendors is arranged first by state or province, then by zip code (to make it easy for readers to locate a nursery near them), then alphabetically by the nursery name. While I've made every effort to make the list as complete and accurate as possible, some suppliers may inadvertently have been omitted, and exact business addresses are notoriously difficult to keep up to date. The fact that a supplier appears on this list is not meant as an endorsement of that supplier.

Some nurseries charge a fee for their catalogs, and sometimes the cost is refundable with the first order. Nurseries that have only lists may ask for one or two first-class stamps.

A key to offerings appears on the facing page. The designation "Iris" means that no specific types are listed in the company's advertising.

UNITED STATES

Arizona

Shepard Iris Garden, 3342 Orangewood, Phoenix, AZ 85051; Catalog, 2 stamps.
TB, Spur

Kary Iris Gardens, 6201 E. Calle Rosa, Scottsdale, AZ 85251.
TB, IB, AB

Master Creations, 3970 N. Hwy. 89, Prescott, AZ 86301; Catalog, $2.
TB

Arkansas

Pine Ridge Gardens, 632-I Sycamore Rd., London, AR 72847; Catalog, $1.
Beardless Iris

California

Cal-Dixie Iris Gardens, 14115 Pear St., Riverside, CA 92508; Catalog, 2 stamps.
TB

Rancho de los Flores, 8000 Balcom Canyon Rd., Somis, CA 93066; Catalog, free.
TB, La, Spur

Sutton's Green Thumber, 16592 Road 208, Porterville, CA 93257; Catalog, $1, refundable with purchase.
TB

Scott's Iris Garden, 14605 Chispa Rd., Atascadero, CA 93422.
TB, IB, DB

Iris Hill Farm, 7280 Tassajara Creek Rd., Santa Margarita, CA 93453.
Iris

Babbette's Gardens, 40975 N. 172 St. E., Lancaster, CA 93535; Catalog, $1.
TB

Napa Country Iris Gardens, 9087 Steele Canyon Rd., Napa, CA 94558; Catalog, 1 stamp.
TB

Messick Garden, 200 Pine Creek Rd., Walnut Creek, CA 94598; no list.
TB

Bay View Gardens, 1201 Bay St., Santa Cruz, CA 95060; Catalog, $2.
TB, La, PCN, Spur

Superstition Iris Gardens, 2536 Old Highway, Cathey's Valley, CA 95306; Catalog, $1.
TB, IB, DB, AB

Iris Lady's Gardens, 2701 Fine Ave., Modesto, CA 95355; Catalog, $1, refundable with purchase.
TB, IB, DB

Nicholson's Woodland Iris Gardens, 2405 Woodland Ave., Modesto, CA 95358; Catalog, $1, refundable with purchase.
TB

O'Brien Iris Garden, 3223 Canfield Rd., Sebastopol, CA 95427; Catalog, $1.
Iris

The Iris Gallery, 33450 Little Valley Rd., Fort Bragg, CA 95437; Catalog, $1.
TB, PCN, Sp

Moonshine Gardens, PO Box 1521, Healdsburg, CA 95448; Catalog, $2, refundable with purchase.
TB

M. A. D. Iris Garden, 4828 Jela Way, North Highlands, CA 95660; Catalog, free.
TB

Rainbow Acres, 3239 i St., North Highlands, CA 95660; no list.
TB

Bluebird Haven Iris Garden, 6940 Fairplay Rd., Somerset, CA 95684; Catalog, $1.
Iris

Lauer's Flowers, 11314 Randolph Rd., Wilton, CA 95693.
Iris

Roris Gardens, 8195 Bradshaw Rd., Sacramento, CA 95829; Catalog, $4, refundable with purchase.
TB

Cabral's Gardens, PO Box 9264, Chico, CA 95927; Catalog, $1, refundable with purchase.
TB

Colorado

Long's Gardens, PO Box 19, Boulder, CO 80306.
TB

Willow Bend Farm, 1154 Hwy 65, Eckert, CO 81418; Catalog, free.
TB

Idaho

Sand Hollow Iris Gardens, 14000 Oasis Rd., Caldwell, ID 83605; Catalog, $2, refundable with purchase.
TB

Enchanted Iris Garden, 715 Central Canyon, Napma, ID 83651; Catalog, $1, refundable with purchase.
Iris

Stanley Iris Garden, 3245 N. Wing Rd., Star, ID 83669; Catalog, $1.
TB

Illinois

Illini Iris, 1690 N. State St., Monticello, IL 61856; Catalog, $2, refundable with purchase.
Sib

Redbud Lane Iris Gardens, Rte. 1, Box 141, Kansas, IL 61933; Catalog, $1.
TB

Indiana

Miller's Manor Gardens, 3167 E. US 224, Ossian, IN 46777; Catalog, $1, refundable with purchase.
TB, Sib

Iowa

David Iris Farm, Rt. 1, Fort Dodge, IA 50501; Catalog, 1 stamp.
TB, IB, DB

Kentucky

Bridge in Time Iris Gardens, 10116 Scottsville Rd., Alvaton, KY 42122; Catalog, 1 stamp.
TB

Louisiana

Bois d'Arc Gardens, 1831 Bull Run Rd., Schriever, LA 70360; Catalog, $2.
La

Louisiana Nursery, 5853 Highway 182, Opelousas, LA 70570; Catalog, $4.
La, JI, Spur, Lv

Maine

Pope's Perennials, 39 Highland Ave., Gorham, ME 04038; Catalog, 1 stamp.
Sib, JI

Eartheart Gardens, RR 1, Box 847, Harpswell, ME 04079; Catalog, 1 stamp.
Sib, JI

Maryland

Draycott Gardens, 16815 Falls Rd., Upperco, MD 21155; Catalog, $1.
Sib, JI

Friendship Gardens, 2490 Wellworth Way, West Friendship, MD 21794; Catalog, $2.
TB

Massachusetts

Fox Brook Iris Farm, 90 Call Rd., Colrain, MA 01340; local only.
Iris

Joe Pye Weed's Garden, 337 Acton St., Carlisle, MA 01741; Catalog, $1.
Sib, Sp

York Hill Farm, 18 Warren St., Georgetown, MA 01833; Catalog, $1.50.
JI, Sib

Hermit Medlars Walk, 3 Pierce St., Foxborough, MA 02305; Catalog, $1, refundable with purchase.
TB, IB, DB

Michigan

Harold R. Stahly, 8343 Manchester Dr., Grand Blanc, MI 48439; no list.
TB, IB

Mill Creek Gardens, 210 Parkway, Lapeer, MI 48446; Catalog, $1, refundable with purchase.
TB, IB, DB, Sib

Arrowhead Alpines, PO Box 857, Fowlerville, MI 48836; Catalog, $2.
Sp

Ensata Gardens, 9823 E. Michigan Ave., Galesburg, MI 49053; Catalog, $2.
JI

Minnesota

Busse Gardens, 13579 10th St. NW, PO Box N, Cokato, MN 55321; Catalog, $2, refundable with purchase.
Sib

Riverdale Iris Gardens, PO Box 524, Rockford, MN 55373; Catalog, $1.
TB, IB, DB, Sib

Cooper's Garden, 2345 Decatur Ave. N., Golden Valley, MN 55427; Catalog, $2.
Sib, La, Sp

Mississippi

Walter A. Moores, Rt. 1, Box 630, Oakland, MS 38948; no list.
TB

Missouri

Nicodemus Iris Gardens, RR 1, Box 297, Buffalo, MO 65622.
TB, IB, La, JI, Spur, Sib

Cape Iris Garden, 822 Rodney Vista, Cape Girardeau, MO 63701; Catalog, $1, refundable with purchase.
TB, IB, DB, Spur

Comanche Acres Iris Gardens, Rte. 1, Box 258, Gower, MO 64454; Catalog, $3.
TB, IB, La

Knee-deep in June, 708 N. 10th St., St. Joseph, MO 64505; no list in 1997.
Iris

Key to iris offerings

TB	Tall Bearded
IB	Intermediate Bearded
DB	Dwarf Bearded
Sib	Siberian
La	Louisiana
JI	Japanese
Lv	Laevigatas (water irises)
Spur	Spurias
Sp	Species
Ar	Arils
AB	Arilbreds
Bb	Bulbous
PCN	Pacific Coast Native

Cher-Den Iris Farm, 29523 Highway 36, Brookfield, MO 64628; Catalog, 1 stamp. TB, IB, DB

Adamgrove, Rte. 1, Box 1472, California, MO 65018; Catalog, $3, refundable with purchase. TB, IB, DB, Sp

Montana

Sourdough Iris Gardens, 109 Sourdough Ridge Rd., Bozeman, MT 59715; Catalog, SASE. TB

Mountain View Gardens, 2435 Middle Rd., Columbia Falls, MT 59912. Sib

Nebraska

Dance-in-the-Wind Iris Garden, 810 S. 14th St., Tekamah, NE 68061; Catalog, $1. TB, IB

Newburn's Iris Gardens, 1415 Meadow Dale Dr., Lincoln, NE 68505; Catalog, free. TB

Varigay Gardens, 7090 Cornhusker Hwy., Lincoln, NE 68507; Catalog, SASE. TB

Maple Tree Gardens, PO Box 547, Ponca, NE 68770; Catalog, $.50. TB

Spruce Gardens, 2317 3rd Rd., Wisner, NE 68791; Catalog, $1, refundable with purchase. TB, IB

Monument Iris Garden, 50029 Sunflower Rd., Mitchell, NE 69357; Catalog, $1, refundable with purchase. TB

North Pine Iris Gardens, PO Box 595, Norfolk, NE 68701; Catalog, $1, refundable with purchase. TB, IB

New Jersey

Fran's Iris Garden, 14 Chestnut Dr., East Windsor, NJ 08520; no list. TB

New Mexico

Pleasure Iris Gardens, 425 E. Luna Azul Dr., Chaparral, NM 88021; Catalog, $1. Ar, AB

McAllister's Iris Gardens, PO Box 112, Fairacres, NM 88033; Catalog, $1, refundable with purchase. AB

The Blooming Place, 1902 E. Pine Lodge Rd., Roswell, NM 88201; Catalog, 1 stamp. Iris

New York

Van Bourgondien, PO Box 1000, Babylon, NY 11702; Catalog, free. Bb

Van Dyck's, PO Box 430, Brightwaters, NY 11718; Catalog, free. Bb

Phoenix Flower Farm, 2620 Lamson, Phoenix, NY 13135; Catalog, $2, refundable with purchase. Iris

Borglum's Iris, 2202 Austin Rd., Geneva, NY 14456; Catalog, 1 stamp. TB, IB, DB, Sib

North Carolina

We-Du Nurseries, Rt. 5, Box 724, Marion, NC 28752; Catalog, $1, refundable with purchase. Sp

North Dakota

Pederson's Iris Patch, Sibley, Dazey, ND 58429; Catalog, 2 stamps. TB

Ohio

Ohio Gardens, 102 Laramie Rd., Marietta, OH 45750; Catalog, $1. IB

Oklahoma

Contemporary Gardens, Box 534, Blanchard, OK 73010; Catalog, $2. TB, IB, La

Mid-America Garden, 3409 N. Geraldine, Oklahoma City, OK 73112; Catalog, $2. Iris

Mountain View Iris Gardens, 6307 Irwin Ave., Lawton, OK 73505; Catalog, free. Iris

Hadaway Farms, Rte. 1, Box 42M, Carney, OK 74832; Catalog, $1, refundable with purchase. TB, IB

Oregon

Fleur de Lis Gardens, 185 NE Territorial Rd., Canby, OR 97013; Catalog, $2, refundable with purchase. TB

Chehalem Gardens, PO Box 693, Newberg, OR 97132; Catalog, free. Sib, Spur

Jim and Vicky Craig, 16325 SW 113 Ave., Tigard, OR 97224; Catalog, 1 stamp. TB, IB, DB

Schreiner's Iris Gardens, 3629 Quinaby Rd., Salem, OR 97303; Catalog, $5, refundable with purchase. TB, IB, DB

Iris Country, 6219 Topaz St. NE, Brooks, OR 97305; no list. TB, Sp

Keith Keppel, PO Box 18154, Salem, OR 97305; Catalog, $2, refundable with purchase. TB, IB, DB

Nature's Garden, 40611 Highway 226, Scio, OR 97374; Catalog, $1, refundable with purchase. JI, Sib, PCN, Sp

Cooley's Gardens, 11553 Silverton Rd. NE, Box 126, Silverton, OR 97381; Catalog, $5, refundable with purchase. TB

D. and J. Gardens, 7872 Prarie Road NE, Silverton, OR 97381; Catalog, $1. TB

Laurie's Garden, 41886 McKenzie Hwy., Springfield, OR 97478; Catalog, 1 stamp. JI, Sib, Lv, Sp

Pennsylvania

Primrose Path, RD 2, Box 110, Scottdale, PA 15683; Catalog, $2. Sp

Sterling & Barbara Innerst, 2700-A Oakland Rd., Dover, PA 17315; no list. TB

George C. Bush, 1739 Memory Lane Ext., York, PA 17402; Catalog, 1 stamp. JI, Sib, Sp

Mount Gretna Gardens, 2493 Pinch Rd., Manheim, PA 17545; Catalog, SASE. La, JI, Sib, Lv, Sp

South Carolina

Pecan Grove Gardens, Gaffney, SC 29341.
TB, IB, Sp, La, JI

Quail Hill Gardens, 2460 Compton Bridge Rd., Inman, SC 29349.
TB, IB, Sp, La, JI, Sib

South Dakota

Foxes' Iris Patch, RR 5, Box 382, Huron, SD 57350; Catalog, $3, refundable with purchase.
TB

Tennessee

Rockytop Gardens, PO Box 41, Eagleville, TN 37060; Catalog, $2.
TB

Iris City Gardens, 502 Brighton Place, Nashville, TN 37205; Catalog, free.
JI, La, Sib, Sp

Stephen's Lane Iris Gardens, Rt 1, Box 136-H, Bells, TN 38006; Catalog, $1.
JI, Sib, Spur, Sp, TB

Texas

Lone Star Iris Gardens, 5637 Saddleback Rd., Garland, TX 75043; Catalog, $2.
La

TB's Place, 1513 Ernie Lane, Grand Prairie, TX 75052.
Iris

Argyle Acres, 910 Pioneer Circle East, Argyle, TX 76226; Catalog, 2 stamps.
TB

Mary's Garden, Rt. 1, Box 348, Hico, TX 76457; Catalog, $2, refundable with purchase.
TB

Utah

Zebra Gardens, 9130 North 5200 West, Elwood, UT 84337.
TB, IB, DB

North Forty Iris, 93 East 100 South, Logan, UT 84321; Catalog, $1, refundable with purchase.
TB

Spanish Fork Iris Garden, 40 South 200 West, Spanish Fork, UT 84660; Catalog, 2 stamps.
TB, IB, AB

Virginia

Nicholls Gardens, 4724 Angus Dr., Gainesville, VA 22065; Catalog, $1, refundable with purchase.
TB, IB, JI, La, Sib, Sp

Winterberry Gardens, 1225 Reynolds Rd., Cross Junction, VA 22625; Catalog, $2.
TB

Andre Viette Farm and Nursery, Rt. 1, Box 16, Fisherville, VA 22939; Catalog, free.
Iris

Daffodil Mart, 7463 Heath Trail, Gloucester, VA 23061; Catalog, free.
Bb

Dan River Gardens, PO Box 707, State Road 632, Meadows of Dan, VA 24120; Catalog, $1, refundable with purchase.
TB

Weikle's Wonderland, PO Box 175, Shawsville, VA 24162; Catalog, $1, refundable with purchase.
TB

Washington

Holland Gardens, 29106 Meridian, East Graham, WA 98338; Catalog, $1.
TB

Aitken's Salmon Creek Garden, 608 NW 119 St., Vancouver, WA 98685; Catalog, $2.
TB

Lorraine's Iris Patch, 20272 Road 11 NW, Quincy, WA 98848; Catalog, free.
TB

Wisconsin

McClure & Zimmerman, 108 W. Winnebago St., Friesland, WI 53935; Catalog, free.
Bb

CANADA

Alberta

Parkland Perennials, Box 3683, Spruce Grove, AB T7X 3A9; Catalog, free.
DB, IB, TB, Sib

British Columbia

Ambrosia Gardens, PO Box 1135, Vernon, BC V1T 6N4; Catalog, $2, refundable with purchase.
Iris

Pacific Rim Native Plants, 44305 Old Orchard Rd., Sardis, BC V2R 1A9.
Sp

Beachwood Daylily and Perennials, Box 60240 Fraser Postal Outlet, Vancouver, BC V5W 4B5; Catalog, $2.
Sib, Spur

Miller Mountain Nursery, 5086 McLay Road, RR3, Duncan, BC V9L 2X1; Catalog, $2.
La, Sp

Ferncliff Gardens, 8394 McTaggart St., Mission, BC V2V 6S6.
DB, TB

Manitoba

F. P. Healey, Box 6, Belmont, MB R0K 0C0; Catalog, $2, refundable with purchase.
TB, Sib, Spur, Ar, Sp

Ontario

Whitehouse Perennials, RR2, Almonte, ON K0A 1A0; Catalog, $3, refundable with purchase.
Sib

McMillen's Iris Garden, RR1, Norwich, ON N0J 1P0; Catalog, $2.
TB, DB, IB, Sib, Spur, Ar

Sipkins Nurseries, 3261 London Line, RR1, Wyoming, ON N0N 1T0; Catalog, free.
DB, IB, Sib, JI, Sp

Chuck Chapman Iris, 8790 Hwy. 24, Guelph, ON N1L 1B1; Catalog, $2, refundable with purchase.
TB, DB, Sib, Spur, JI, Ar, Sp

Quebec

Iris Plus, 1269 Rte. 139, Box 903, Sutton, QC J0E 2K0; Catalog, $2, refundable with purchase.
TB, DB, IB, Sib, JI

Les Jardins Osiris, 818 Rue Monique, CP 489, St.-Thomas, QC J0K 3L0; Catalog, $2, refundable with purchase.
Sib, JI

Books and Computer Resources

This book is intended as no more than an introduction to the vast subject of the genus *Iris*. For readers wanting to delve more deeply into the subject, a wide variety of detailed information is available in print and electronic formats.

Books

Caillet, Marie, and Joseph K. Mertsweiller, eds. *The Louisiana Iris.* Waco, Tex.: The Society for Louisiana Irises and Texas Gardener Press, 1988.

This book has chapters by a number of different authorities on Louisiana Irises and a large number of color and monochrome photographs throughout. Particularly good are the chapters with cultural advice targeted to specific regions of North America, as well as Australia and Japan.

Cassidy, G. E., and S. Linnegar. *Growing Irises.* Portland, Ore.: Timber Press, 1982.

This book was written in 1982 by two prominent members of the British Iris Society. It is organized according to the garden uses of irises, with chapter titles like "Irises in the Mixed Border" and "Irises for the Bulb Frame and the Alpine House." The focus is definitely horticultural, with a good deal of sage advice—but intended for the British gardener. There are some nice line drawings, but relatively few color illustrations.

Dykes, William Rickatson. *The Genus Iris.* New York: Dover Publications, 1975.

The great classic of iris literature, made available as an inexpensive, large-format reprint, this is a species-by-species account, but the botanical descriptions are highly readable and contain many incidental gems of information. The essays on cultivation and breeding that accompany many of the species accounts are very valuable. There are many excellent line drawings and 48 superb color plates (color drawings, not photographs). If you're serious about irises, you need this book.

Köhlein, Fritz. *Iris.* Portland, Ore.: Timber Press, 1987.

This is a translation of a 1981 German book; it's about 375 pages long. Köhlein spends a good deal of space on a species-by-species account, but the horticultural material here is more extensive than in Brian Mathew's *The Iris,* and more attention is paid to garden hybrids.

This book was intended for readers in Germany, so the cultural advice has to be read with that in mind. There is an extensive section on hybridizing, written by Peter Werckmeister, which is fairly technical and probably not useful for the average gardener.

The color illustrations are excellent and show a wide variety of iris types, usually in a garden setting or their natural habitat. Americans will recognize only one or two of the Bearded Iris varieties pictured. I have never seen the original German version, but the translation seems clumsy in places, and sometimes makes no sense at all.

Mathew, Brian. *The Iris.* New York: Universe Books, 1981.

This book, a popular account in some 200 pages by a noted botanist, first appeared in the United States in 1981, and there has since been a second edition, though little of importance to the gardener was changed.

Each section of *Iris* is taken up species by species, with detailed descriptions of the plants and their native habitats. Horticultural varieties, however, are given short shrift. The cultural advice is brief and focuses on Britain, so American readers need to be aware of the differences in conditions between there and here. Many of the color illustrations show irises in their native habitats, and the line drawings are superb. As a writer, Mathew knows how to put in just enough personal detail to create interest. An excellent reference, and my second favorite book on irises.

McEwen, Currier. *The Japanese Iris.* Hanover, N. H.: University Press of New England, 1990.

A companion volume toMcEwen's *The Siberian Iris* (see below), and written along the same general plan. About 30 color pictures.

McEwen, Currier. *The Siberian Iris.* Portland, Ore.: Timber Press, 1996.

This book will be the last word for some time to come on Siberian Irises. Dr. McEwen, at this writing still active in his mid-90s, has been a leader for years in breeding Siberian Irises. The style of the book is straightforward and readable, and much information on culture is included. The color plates are mostly species and varietal portraits.

Species Group of the British Iris Society, eds. *A Guide to Species Irises, Their Identification and Cultivation.* Cambridge, England: Cambridge University Press, 1997.

As the name suggests, this 365-page book is a species-by-species account of the genus, with very brief introductory chapters on general topics—the chapter on cultivation is less than four pages long. The species descriptions are technical, botanical, and rather dry, and cultural notes appended to each tend to be short. There are nice line drawings of many species, but the uninspired (and relatively few) color illustrations are of uneven quality.

Waddick, James W., and Zhao Yu-tang. *Irises of China.* Portland, Ore.: Timber Press, 1992.

The first part of this book is an informal account by Waddick of the Iris species found in China, with extensive notes on their cultivation. The color-photograph section includes pictures of irises not seen elsewhere, but the quality of the pictures is uneven.

The second half is a reprint of Zhao's highly technical volume on Irises from *Flora Reipublicae Popularis Sinicae,* illustrated with finely executed line drawings. This book will become more important when more Chinese species make their way into cultivation.

Warburton, Bee, and Melba Hamblen, eds. *The World of Irises.* Salt Lake City: Publishers Press, 1978. Available only from the American Iris Society.

This comprehensive book of nearly 500 pages covers every conceivable iris subject, including culture, genetics, and history. But since it first appeared, much has happened. An updated version is in the works, but may not appear for several years.

I consider this the Iris "Bible," and my copy is nearly worn out from constant use. It's clearly the best book on irises ever produced. However, the color illustrations are unimaginative and small.

COMPUTER RESOURCES

Computer software specifically to store records of iris collections is available from B. B. Iris, 669 Peoria St., No. 118, Aurora, CO 80011. Requires Windows 3.1 or Windows 95, 386 CPU, 6 megs RAM, 1.4 floppy disk. $24.95 for Windows 3.1, $29.95 for Windows 95; $6.00 shipping and handling in either case.

The American Iris Society maintains a World Wide Web page at www.isomedia.com/homes/AIS. From here you can access many other web pages devoted to irises of various kinds, as well as the web pages of a number of commercial iris growers.

IRIS-L is an electronic mail list that will keep you informed on all manner of things relating to irises. To join IRIS-L, send the e-mail message SUBSCRIBE IRIS-L *your name* (add your own name here) to listserv@rt66.com. You will get a return message with instructions and the rules of the list, and can begin to participate immediately.

INDEX

patterns of 105-106
pests of, 113-114
planting, 110-11
Juno Irises:
  discussed, 23, 97-98
  growing, 98-100
  propagating, 100

L

Laevigatas, described, 19-20
Leaf miners, control of, 86
Leaf spots, discussed, 51-52, 133
Louisiana Irises:
  bloom season of, 82
  cultural requirements of, 80-85
  discussed, 18, 74-75
  diseases of, 86
  dividing, 85
  flowers of, described, 76-77
  hybridization of, 79
  mulching, 84
  pests of, 86-87
  planting, 83-84
  plants of, described, 75-76
  propagating, 86
  species of, 77-78
  tetraploid, 79
Luminata, defined, 27

M

Miniature Dwarfs, described, 11-12,
    30-31
Miniature Talls, described, 12, 13,
    30-31
Mulching:
  discussed, 44
  of Siberian Irises, 67

N

Nematodes:
  beneficial, 56-57
  as pests, 41, 113
Nurseries, iris, listed, 162-65

P

Pacific Coast Native Irises:
  cultural requirements of, 141-43
  discussed, 17-18, 140-43
  hybrids of, 141
  See also Calsibes.

'Paltec,' profiled, 137-38
Penicillium rot, discussed, 101
Pests:
  preventing, 51
  See also individual pests.
Planting, sequence of, 41-43
Plicata, defined, 27

R

Replanting:
  bed preparation for, 46
  process of, 48, 49
Reticulata Irises:
  discussed, 22-23, 93, 95
  growing, 96-97
Rhizome rot, discussed, 86, 133
Rhizomes:
  planting, 42-43
  role of, 8-9

S

Sclerotium rot, discussed, 101
Scorch, discussed, 53, 71
Seeds, iris:
  described, 147
  planting, 148
  sources for, 148
  starting indoors, 149
Self, defined, 25
Siberian Irises:
  blooming season of, 62
  as border plants, 64
  characteristics of, 58-59
  color of, 61
  cultural requirements of, 63-68
  described, 17
  diseases of, 70-71
  dividing, 68-70
  pattern of, 61-62
  pests of, 71
  planting, 66
    seasons for, 64
  Sino-Siberians, 60, 71-73
  sources for, 63
  subseries of, 60
Slugs, control of, 87
Snails, control of, 87
Snake's Head Iris, profiled, 96
Soil, amending, 40
Solarization, for bed preparation, 40
Spanish Irises:
  characteristics of, 23, 89-90
  cultural requirements of, 91-92

Spuria Irises:
  care of, 125
  cultural requirements of, 123-26
  described, 16-17, 120-23
  diseases of, 126-27
  pests of, 127
  planting, 124
Standard, defined, 6
Standard Dwarfs, described, 12, 30-31

T

Tall Bearded Irises:
  bloom season of, 32
  care of, 44-45
  colors of, 27-28
  described, 12-14, 30-31
  form of, 28-29
  most popular, 159
Tetraploid, defined, 34-35
Thrips, control of, 114

V

Variegata, defined, 27
Vesper Iris, profiled, 142

W

Whiteflies, control of, 53
Winter Iris. *See Iris unguicularis.*

X

Xiphium Irises:
  discussed, 23, 89
  growing, 91-93
  See also Dutch Irises. English Irises.
      Spanish Irises.

Y

Yellowing foliage, discussed, 71

Book publisher: Jim Childs

Associate publisher: Helen Albert

Editorial assistant: Cherilyn DeVries

Editor: Ruth Dobsevage

Designer / Layout artist: Henry Roth

Illustrator: John H. Hartley, Jr.

Indexer: Peter Chapman

Typeface: Berling

Paper: 80-lb. Utopia Two Gloss, neutral pH

Printer: R. R. Donnelley, Willard, Ohio

Photographers:

David Cavagnaro: p. 139 right

John Coble: pgs. 105 bottom, 114

Derek Fell: pgs. 22, 95 bottom, 116 left

Roger Foley: pgs. 12,13 top right and bottom, 16, 17, 18 top, 20 bottom, 21 bottom, 23, 25, 26 bottom, 27 left, 29, 32 right, 33, 41, 42, 43, 47, 48, 59, 61, 62, 65 top, 66, 68, 69, 70, 75, 76 right, 78 left, 79 right, 81, 89, 98, 105 top, 106 bottom, 107 top left and bottom, 109, 111, 112, 115, 117, 119 left, 121, 122, 124, 125, 126, 132, 135, 136 right, 140 left, 147, 151, 155 right, 157, back cover (top left and right), spine

Mick Hales: p. 63

Pamela Harper: pgs. 90 left, 95 top, 96, 103 top, 142, 144, back cover (middle)

Carla Lankow: pgs. 72 bottom left, 136 left, 139 left, 143 left

Mike Lowe: pgs. 5, 13 top left, 14, 27 right, 35, 65 bottom, 72 top, 116 right, 129 right, 140 right, 148, 153, 156, back cover (bottom)

Charles Mann: p. 18 bottom

Brian Mathew: pgs. 94, 100

Sharon McAllister: pgs. 15, 129 left

William Shear: pgs. 6, 11, 19, 20 top, 21 top, 26 top, 52, 55, 56, 60, 72 bottom right, 76 left, 77, 78 right, 79 left, 90 right, 93, 103 bottom, 106 top, 107 top right, 118, 119 right, 130 right, 137, 138, 143 right, 155 left

George Waters: pgs. 32 left, 73, 130 left